Architectural Books
in Early America

Architectural Books in Early America

Architectural Treatises and Building Handbooks Available in American Libraries and Bookstores through 1800

Janice G. Schimmelman

Oak Knoll Press
New Castle, Delaware
1999

First Edition, second printing, revised and expanded.

Published by **Oak Knoll Press**
310 Delaware Street, New Castle DE 19720

Originally published in 1986 by the American Antiquarian Society Proceedings, vol. 95, part 2 under the title: *Architectural Treatises and Building Handbooks Available in American Libraries and Bookstores through 1800.*

ISBN: 1-884718-99-X

Title: Architectural Books in Early America
Author: Janice G. Schimmelman
Typographer: J. Schimmelman
Publication Director: J. Lewis von Hoelle
Cover design: J. von Hoelle/ M. Hohne

Copyright   1999 Janice G. Schimmelman

Library of Congress Cataloging-in-Publication Data

Schimmelman, Janice Gayle.
    Architectural books in early America : architectural treaties and building handbooks available in American libraries and bookstores through 1800 / Janice G. Schimmelman. -- 1st ed.
      p.   cm.
    "Originally published in 1986 by the American Antiquarian Society proceedings, vol. 95, part 2 under the title: Architectural treatises and building handbooks available in American libraries and bookstores through 1800"--T.p. verso.
    Includes bibliographical references and index.
    ISBN 1-884718-99-X (hb)
    1. Architecture--History Bibliography. 2. Early printed books--17th century Bibliography. 3. Early printed books--18th century Bibliography. 4. United States--Imprints. I. Title.
Z5941.S43 1999
016.72--dc21   99-26451
                                                                            CIP

ALL RIGHTS RESERVED:
No part of this book may be reproduced in any manner without the express written consent of the publisher, except in the case of brief excepts in critical reviews and articles. All inquiries should be addressed to: Oak Knoll Press, 310 Delaware Street, New Castle, DE 19720

Printed in the United States of America on 60# archival, acid-free paper.

To John Browning Cameron

TABLE OF CONTENTS

FOREWORD v

PREFACE ix

INTRODUCTION 1

CHECKLIST 6

APPENDIX A 163

   Publication Dates and Imprints of Books
   Cited, in Order of Number of References

APPENDIX B 177

   Treatises Listed by Date of Earliest American
   Catalogue Reference

APPENDIX C 184

   Treatises Listed Alphabetically by Individual
   Library or Firm

APPENDIX D 206

   Libraries and Booksellers Listed in Order of
   the Size of Their Collections

BIBLIOGRAPHY 211

INDEX TO CHECKLIST 213

FOREWORD

Architectural Books in Early America is as comprehensive a list as currently possible of architectural books that were in America from Colonial times to the Republic, from the late seventeenth century, when British colonists in America first might need such books, to the seminal year of Jefferson's election, 1800, by which time the nation had been formed, polarized within, and prepared to expand.

It is valuable in several different ways. As a book about books it is a useful resource that updates the classic on American architectural books up to the Revolution by Helen Park (1961) and Henry-Russell Hitchcock's earlier bibliography up to 1895 (1946). Like Park's, Janice G. Schimmelman's book began in print as an article. It was originally published in the *Proceedings of the American Antiquarian Society* (1986). Revised and expanded, it is an essential tool for the collector or student of books on early American architecture.

Architectural Books in Early America is also a rich resource for social and cultural historians, for the books it lists were highly influential in American business and the built landscape. For the most part the publication of these building handbooks parallels periods of extraordinary growth, first in the colonies in the 1760s and later in the Federalist years of the United States in the 1790s. We often think of historic architectural books as picture books of style. They were often that but just as often were guides by which a builder could learn, step by step, how he might profit using the latest technology and fashion.

Architectural and decorative style are still the main attractions of the handbooks today, for they are sometimes valuable in determining the design sources for surviving structures. It is believed that George Washington in his development of Mount Vernon referred for models and ideas to Batty Langley's *The City and Country Builder's and Workman's Treasury of Designs* (1746). In her research Schimmelman located one of the British editions in a Philadelphia library catalogue, and others advertised for sale in the catalogues of booksellers in Philadelphia, Boston and New York.

The importance of the iconography in these books in shaping America's formal architecture and its many spin-offs is more than can be closely assessed. In studying the finer eighteenth-century buildings, the suggestion of the presence of the books is always strong, even when specific books cannot be picked out. George Washington, who loved building, again as an example, was intimate with the design of the White House. Thwarted in his effort to build a really palatial building, he seems to have settled down by 1792 to the idea of what the English would call a "gentleman's house," meaning a substantial country house. In selling the President on the idea of modeling the building on the stately, if old-fashioned house of the Duke of Leinster in Kildare Street, Dublin, architect James Hoban almost certainly showed him plates of the house from Robert Pool and John Cash's *Views of the Most Remarkable Public Buildings, Monuments and Other Edifices in the City of Dublin* (1780). Washington adopted the model and ordered Hoban to add carved stone embellishments far beyond the original. Hoban, who attended the Royal Dublin Society's drawing school in the time when Pool and Cash were students there, probably had his own copy. Schimmelman finds two of these books offered for sale a few years later, one at the venerable bookshop and publishing house of Mathew Carey in Philadelphia, 1794, and the other at Ross and Douglas, booksellers, Petersburg, Virginia, 1800.

Geometry and mathematics are as much a presence in most of the books as plans and elevations. They gain far less attention, if any, from scholars, but to the field of historic restoration, they are significant to understanding how the buildings were built. This mysterious subject of construction is only today beginning to be explored by builders, conservators and historians, as the detrimental results of modern building solutions become more and more evident in restorations completed over the past thirty years.

It is easy enough to admire and study the line illustrations. But comprehending the diagrams, as well as the text about the how-to of building in these volumes can be a real task, not always with fruitful results. Yet the more one reads, the clearer they become. Among the more famous American-born guide books is Asher Benjamin's *The Country Builder's Assistant* which appeared first in the late eighteenth century and popularized the neoclassical taste of Bulfinch's Boston. Benjamin focused more on building than design. He hoped in his book's subtitle that his "new designs of carpentry and architecture" would be "particularly useful to country workmen." And indeed his ideas and techniques were carried via his many books from New England all across the American frontier to the Pacific. His way of making doors, measuring to cut wood, planning the joinery of window sash, roof-framing—myriad details, were incorporated in countless buildings.

Janice G. Schimmelman's book recommends itself by giving general and convenient access to her worthy scholarship. She improves upon and brings to the present day research labors of previous scholars, yet provides a book quite her own. *Architectural Books in Early America* is a timepiece for architectural scholars and an index for those who study construction practices.

William Seale,
Alexandria, Virginia

PREFACE

I would like to thank Dr. Frank H. Sommer, former Head of Library at the Winterthur Museum, for his assistance while consulting the museum's collection of architectural treatises and building handbooks. I would also like to thank Dr. Charles E. Brownell for introducing me to architectural pattern books and to the significant role they played in the development of eighteenth-century English and American architecture.

This checklist of architectural treatises and building handbooks was originally published in the *Proceedings of the American Antiquarian Society* 95 (October 1985): 317-500. It has been reprinted with the kind permission of the American Antiquarian Society. The introduction has been modified and a bibliography and index have been added. The checklist and appendices, however, remain unchanged.

Support for this project was provided by a Travel to Collections Grant from the National Endowment for the Humanities and a Research Grant from Oakland University.

Architectural Books in Early America

INTRODUCTION

Helen Park produced the first major study of European architectural treatises and handbooks in eighteenth-century America. Her research, published as *A List of Architectural Books Available in America Before the Revolution*, identified 106 European architectural books that were either owned by private individuals or libraries, or sold by bookstores before 1776.[1] Park's work not only identified the possible stylistic sources of eighteenth-century American architecture but also enhanced our understanding of colonial dependence upon British culture and the printed word.

The purpose of this present checklist is twofold: to develop a list of European architectural books available in America through 1800 and to identify eighteenth-century libraries and bookstores which either circulated or sold architectural books. My intention has been to enhance, clarify, and expand Park's work by including materials available after the Revolution, a period which experienced a significant increase in the book trade. However, not all books listed by Park are listed here. For example, books on the art of perspective or books owned by private collectors such as William Buckland, Peter Harrison, Mather Byles, William Byrd II and Thomas Jefferson have not been included although they formed part of the Park List.[2]

The checklist which follows identifies 147 architectural treatises and building handbooks available in American libraries or advertised in booksellers' catalogues through 1800; 65 of which are additions to the Park List, the most noteworthy being John Norman's *The Town and Country Builder's Assistant* and four works by William Pain: *The Practical Builder*, *The Carpenter's Pocket Directory*, *Pain's British*

Architectural Books in Early America

Palladio and *The Practical House Carpenter*.

Although it would be impossible to identify every title or locate every copy of an architectural treatise or handbook in early America, one can at least estimate the value of architectural books to the general public and assess the popularity of certain books based upon their appearance in library and booksellers' catalogues. For example, it is quite clear that Francis Price's *The British Carpenter* and Batty Langley's *The Builder's Jewel* were the handbooks listed most frequently in American book catalogues (see Appendix A). On the other hand, Roland Fréart's *Parallele de l'architecture et de la moderne* and Inigo Jones' *The Most Notable Antiquity of Great Britain* were the first architectural books identified as being in America. Both were listed in Duncan Cambell's 1693 catalogue of *The Library of the Late and Learned Mr. Samuel Lee* (see Appendix B). The largest permanent collection of architectural books, however, was owned by the Library Company of Philadelphia, followed at a considerable distance by the New York Society Library and the Baltimore Library Company. Not only did New York and Philadelphia have impressive libraries, they were the best cities in which to buy books on architecture. Those individuals interested in architecture would have been able to purchase a variety of titles at the bookstores of James Rivington and Samuel Brown in New York and Philadelphia, John Ward Fenno in New York, David Hall in Philadelphia, Robert Bell in Philadelphia, Thomas Bradford in Philadelphia, and Garrat Noel and Ebenezer Hazard in New York (see Appendices C & D).

Like all scholars, I stand on the shoulders of those who came before me. In addition to Park's pioneering work, this checklist owes a debt to a number of published sources. The most important by far was the *Early American Imprints, 1639-1800 Series*, edited by Clifford K. Shipton and indexed by

Charles Evans in *American Bibliography* and by Roger P. Bristol in his *Supplement to Charles Evans' American Bibliography*. The microprints published by the American Antiquarian Society provided access to the vast collection of materials printed in America through 1800. The task of identifying the book catalogues available in the *Early American Imprints* was made possible through Robert Winans' *A Descriptive Checklist of Book Catalogues Separately Printed in America 1693-1800*. Biographical information on eighteenth-century American booksellers also has been taken from Winans' publication. In addition, Marcus A. McCorison's *The 1764 Catalogue of the Redwood Library Company at Newport, Rhode Island* and Phillip M. Johnston's M.A. thesis 'A Checklist of Books Relating to Architecture and the Decorative Arts Available in Philadelphia in the Three Decades Following 1780' provided material which helped to clarify a number of citations.

Information on the architectural books themselves came from a variety of sources. With few exceptions all books were consulted either at the library of the Winterthur Museum or at the University of Michigan. Published sources, however, were also valuable including John Archer's *The Literature of British Architecture 1715-1842*, Howard Colvin's *A Biographical Dictionary of British Architects 1600-1840*, the *Catalog of the Avery Memorial Architectural Library*, *The Fowler Architectural Collection of The Johns Hopkins University* and *The National Union Catalog, Pre-1956 Imprints*. Finally, Henry Russell-Hitchcock's *American Architectural Books: A List of Books, Portfolios, and Pamphlets on Architecture and Related Subjects Published in America Before 1895* provided information on American printings of European publications.

This checklist is arranged alphabetically by treatise. Each book is given its first edition title unless otherwise indicated.

English translations and variant titles are also listed when applicable. Park and Hitchcock numbers correspond to their respective publications. Each numbered entry is followed by the libraries or booksellers who listed architectural books in separately published catalogues. Each reference represents the earliest catalogue in which an architectural book appeared. If a bookseller offered a book in more than one list during his years of operation, additional catalogue dates are identified. Such copies, however, are counted only 'once' in the appendices that follow.

Anomalies do occur. Separate entries have been made for the Association Library Company, Union Library Company and the Library Company of Philadelphia even though they merged in 1769. Booksellers may appear more than once if they formed partnerships, for example, James Rivington appears twice, as an individual in 1760 and with Samuel Brown in 1762. Booksellers who listed their latest imports in American newspapers have not been included. They are beyond the scope of this study. Johnston, however, gives us at least a glimpse into the wealth of material contained in eighteenth-century American newspapers by carefully recording which newspapers in Philadelphia advertised books on architecture.

Individual references to architectural books have not been altered. They appear here as they appeared in the eighteenth-century catalogues with their variations in printing and spelling. However, additional information such as place and date of publication or volume size has been arranged in a consistent manner. Following the ¶ symbol, full bibliographical information is given for each initial eighteenth-century catalogue reference. This is followed by the *Early American Imprint* (EAI) number identified by Charles Evans' (E) *American Bibliography*, and Winans' (W) *Checklist* number. A typical entry after the first catalogue reference would thus read

EAI: E22545; W117.

The following checklist, therefore, identifies American booksellers and libraries that either advertised or owned architectural treatises or building handbooks through 1800 and who published the inventories of their holdings as separate catalogues. It is hoped that it will further our understanding of the European and British sources of American architecture and will stimulate continued interest in the architectural publications available in eighteenth-century America.

---

1. Park's work was originally published as ' A List of Architectural Books Available in America Before the Revolution,' *Journal of the Society of Architectural Historians* 20 (October 1961): 115-30. The article was revised and published as *A List of Architectural Books Available in America Before the Revolution* (Los Angeles: Hennessey & Ingalls, Inc., 1973). Items in the Park List are numbered 1-87, 101-119.

2. For a list of European books on perspective available in America before 1800 see Janice G. Schimmelman, 'Books on Drawing and Painting Techniques Available in Eighteenth-Century American Libraries and Bookstores,' *Winterthur Portfolio* 19 (Summer/Autumn 1984): 193-205.

CHECKLIST

1. Adam, Robert (1721-92) & James Adams (1732-1794). *The works in architecture of Robert and James Adam, esquires. Ouvrages d'architecture de Robert et Jacques Adam, ecuyers.* 3 vols. London, 1773-1822. (65cm) Park 1

   Guild, Benjamin (1749-92), bookseller, Boston, Mass.
   Adam's Designs in Architecture. 2 vols. Folio. ¶ *A catalogue of a large assortment of books* ([Boston, 1787?]), p. [3]. EAI: E22545; W117

   Philadelphia, Pa., Library Company
   Architecture (The works in) by Robert and James Adams, with Explanations. London, 1773. Folio. ¶ *The second part of the catalogue* (Philadelphia: Aitken, 1775), p. [6]. EAI: E14392; W93

2. Alberti, Leone Battista (1404-72). *L'architettura di Leonbatista Alberti. Tradotta in lingua fiorentina da Cosimo Bartoli gentil'homo & accademico fiorentino. Con la aggiunta de disegni.* Firenze, 1550. First Latin edition, 1485; first Italian edition, Venice, 1546. (34.5cm)

   Harvard College Library, Cambridge, Mass.
   Alberti (di Leon-Baptista) Architettura. Firenze, 1550. Folio. ¶ *Catalogus librorum bibliothecae* (Boston: Green, 1723), p. 2. EAI: E2432; W8

3. Anderson, James (1739-1808). *A practical treatise on chimneys. Containing full directions for preventing or removing smoke in houses. Illustrated with copperplates.* Edinburgh,

1776. (17.5cm)

Carey, Mathew (1760-1839), bookseller, Philadelphia, Pa.
Anderson on sm[o]ky chimnies. ¶ *Mathew Carey, ... has imported from London, Dublin, and Glasgow, an extensive assortment of books* ([Philadelphia: Carey, 1793]), p. 12.   EAI: E25253; W170

Philadelphia, Pa., Library Company
 A treatise on chimnies; containing directions for preventing or removing smoke in houses; with plates. Edinburgh, 1776. Duodecimo. ¶ *A catalogue of the books belonging to the Library Company of Philadelphia* (Philadelphia: Poulson, 1789), p. 254.
              EAI: E22066; W131

4. Benjamin, Asher (1773-1845). *The country builder's assistant: containing a collection of new designs of carpentry and architecture; which will be particularly useful, to country workmen in general. Illustrated with new and useful designs of frontispieces, chimney pieces, &c. Tuscan, Doric, Ionic, and Corinthian orders, with their bases, capitals, and entablatures: architraves for doors, windows, and chimneys: cornices, base, and surbase mouldings for rooms: doors, and sashes, with their mouldings: the construction of stairs, with their ramps and twist rails: plan, elevation, and one section of a meetinghouse, with the pulpit at large: plans and elevations of houses: the best method of finding the length, and backing of hip rafters: also, the tracing of groins, angle brackets, circular soffits in circular walls, &c. Correctly engraved on thirty copper plates: with a printed explanation to each.* Greenfield, Mass., 1797. (21.5 x 28cm)   Hitchcock 111-14

Hanover, N.H., Hanover Bookstore
   Country Builder's Assistant; Correctly engraved on thirty-seven Copperplates, with explanations to each, by Asher Benjamin. Small quarto. ¶ *Catalogue of books, for sale at the bookstore in Hanover* ([Boston], 1799), p. 9.   EAI: E48868; W264

Thomas, Isaiah (1749-1831), & Ebenezer Turrell Andrews (1766-1851), booksellers, Boston, Mass.
   Country Builder's Assistant; correctly engraved on thirty-seven copperplates, with explanations to each, by Asher Benjamin. Small quarto. ¶ *Catalogue of books, (American editions) for sale at the bookstore of Thomas & Andrews* (Boston, 1799), p. 9.   EAI: E36416; W270

West, David (1765-1810), bookseller, Boston, Mass.
   Country Builder's Assistant; Correctly engraved on thirty-seven Copperplates, with explanations to each, by Asher Benjamin. Small quarto. ¶ *Catalogue of books, printed and published in America and for sale at the bookstore of David West* (Boston, 1799), p. 9.
   EAI: E36701; W272

5. *The builder's dictionary: or, gentleman and architect's companion. Explaining not only the terms of art in all the several parts of architecture, but also containing the theory and practice of the various branches thereof, requisite to be known by masons, carpenters, joiners, bricklayers, plaisterers, painters, glaizers, smiths, turners, carvers, statuaries, plumbers, &c. Also necessary problems in arithmetic, geometry, mechanics, perspective, hydraulics, and other mathematical sciences. Together with the quantities, proportions, and prices of all kinds of materials used in building; with*

Architectural Books in Early America

directions for chusing, preparing, and using them: the several proportions of the five orders of architecture, and all their members, according to Vitruvius, Palladio, Scamozzi, Vignola, M. Le Clerc, &c. With rules for the valuation of houses, and the expence calculated of erecting any fabrick, great or small. The whole illustrated with more than two hundred figures, many of them curiously engraven on copper-plates: bring a work of great use, not only to artificers, but likewise to gentlemen, and others, concerned in building, &c. Faithfully digested from the most approved writers on these subjects. In two volumes. London, 1734. (20cm)

Park 4

Bell, Robert (1731?-84), bookseller, Philadelphia, Pa.
Builder's Dictionary, Also, necessary Problems in the Arts connected with Architecture. 2 vols. ¶ *Just published and now selling . . . a catalogue of a large collection of new and old books* (Philadelphia: Bell, 1783), p. 21. EAI: E17830; W99

Bradford, William (1719-91), auctioneer, Philadelphia, Pa.
Builders Dictionary. 2 vols. ¶ *A catalogue of books. Just imported from London* ([Philadelphia: Bradford, 1760?]), p. 7. Advertised for sale again in 1760 (E41433). EAI: E8555; W34

Carey, Mathew (1760-1839), bookseller, Philadelphia, Pa.
Builder's dictionary, or gentleman and architect's companion, explaining not only the terms of art in all the several parts of architecture, but also containing the theory and practice of the various branches thereof, requisite to masons, carpenters, joiners, bricklayers, &c. &c. &c. 2 vols. Octavo. ¶ *Matthew Carey's cata-*

logue of books (Philadelphia: [Carey], March 12, 1794), p. 61. EAI: E26730; W185

Charleston, S.C., Library Society
Builder's Dictionary. 2 vols. London, 1734. Octavo. ¶ *A catalogue of books, belonging to the incorporated Charlestown Library Society* (Charlestown: Wells, 1770), p. 17. EAI: E11596; W73

Hall, David (1714-72), bookseller, Philadelphia, Pa.
Builder's Dictionary. Octavo. ¶ *Imported in the last ships from London, . . . the following books* ([Philadelphia: Franklin & Hall, 1754]), broadside. Advertised for sale again in 1760 and 1761.
EAI: E40686; W21

Lancaster, Pa., Juliana Library Company
The Builder's Dictionary; or, Architect's Companion; explaining the terms of art in all parts of architecture, with the theory and practice of the various branches requisite to be known in that useful art; illustrated with above two hundred figures and curious copperplates. 2 vols. London, 1734. Octavo. ¶ *The charter, laws, catalogue of books, . . . of the Juliana Library-Company, in Lancaster* (Philadelphia: Hall & Sellers, 1766), pp. 39-40. EAI: E10350; W58

Newport, R.I., Redwood Library
Builder's Dictionary. 2 vols. Octavo. ¶*A catalogue of the books belonging to the Company of the Redwood-Library, in Newport, on Rhode-Island* (Newport: Hall, 1764), p. 18. EAI: E9764; W50

New York, N.Y., Society Library
　Builder's dictionary, or architect's companion. 2 vols. Octavo. ¶*A farther continuation of the catalogue of books belonging to the New-York Society Library* (New York: Swords, 1792), p. 111.　　　EAI: E24610; W163

Philadelphia, Pa., Library Company
　The Builder's Dictionary, or Gentleman's and Architect's Companion; containing the Theory and Practice of the various Branches of Architecture, together with the Quantities and Proportions of all Kinds of Materials, and Directions for chusing and preparing them; Rules for the Valuation of Houses, and the Expence calculated of erecting any Building, great or small. . . . Illustrated with 200 Figures, many of them on Copper Plates. 2 vols. London, 1734. Octavo. ¶*A catalogue of books belonging to the Library Company of Philadelphia* (Philadelphia: Franklin, 1741), pp. 31-32.
　　　　　　　　　　　　　　　　　EAI: E4787; W15

Rivington, James (1724-1802), bookseller, New York, N.Y., & Philadelphia, Pa.
　The Builder's Dictionary, or Architect's Companion, explaining the Theory and Practice of the various Branches of Masons, Carpenters, Joiners, Bricklayers, Plaisterers, Painters, Glaizers, Smiths, Turners, Carvers, Plumbers, with the Quantities and Proportions of all Kinds of Materials used in Building, Directions for chusing, preparing and using them, with Rules for the Valuation of Houses, &c. illustrated with 200 Copper Plates. ¶*A catalogue of books, lately imported, and sold by James Rivington* (New York: Gaine, 1760), p. 46.
　　　　　　　　　　　　　　　　　DeWint; W41

Rivington, James (1724-1802), & Samuel Brown (fl. 1755-69), booksellers, New York, N.Y., & Philadelphia, Pa.
The Builder's Dictionary, or Architect's Companion, explaining the Theory and Practice of the various Branches, of Masons, Carpenters, Joiners, Bricklayers, Plaisterers, Painters, Glazers, Smiths, Turners, Carvers, Plumbers, with the Quantities and Proportions of all Kinds of Materials used in Building, Directions for chusing, preparing and using them, with Rules for the Valuation of Houses, &c. Illustrated with 200 Copper Plates. ¶ *A catalogue of books, sold by Rivington and Brown* ([Philadelphia?], 1762), p. 68.

EAI: E9259; W45

6. *The builders price-book; containing a correct list of the prices allowed by the most eminent surveyors in London, to the several artificers concerned in building. A new edition, corrected, with additions. By an experienced surveyor.* London, 1785. (17.5cm)

Larkin, Ebenezer (1767-1813), bookseller, Boston, Mass.
Builder's Price Book. Octavo. ¶ *Ebenezer Larkin's catalogue of books, for sale* (Boston: [Thomas & Andrews], 1793), p. 45.

EAI: E46803 (no copy reproduced), MiU-C; W176

Thomas, Isaiah (1749-1831), & Ebenezer Turrell Andrews (1766-1851), booksellers, Boston, Mass.
Builder's Price Book. Octavo. ¶ *Thomas and Andrews's catalogue of books, for sale* (Boston: Thomas & Andrews, 1793), p. 45.   EAI: E26252; W181

Architectural Books in Early America

7. Campbell, Colin (1676-1729). *Vitruvius britannicus; or the British architect, containing the plans, elevations, and sections of the regular buildings, both publick and private, in Great Britain, with variety of new designs; in 200 large folio plates, engraven by the best hands; and drawn either from the buildings themselves, or the original designs of the architects; in II volumes. Vitruvius britannicus; ou l'architecte britannique, contenant les plans, elevations, & sections des bâtimens reguliers, tant particuliers que publics de la Grande Bretagne, compris en 200 grandes planches gravez en taille douce par les meilleurs maitres, et tous ou dessinez des bâtimens memes, ou copiez des desseins originaux des architectes: en deux tomes.* 5 vols. London, 1715-71. (51cm)
   Park 5

Harvard College Library, Cambridge, Mass.
   Campbel (Colin) Vitruvius Britannicus. 3 vols. London. Folio. ¶ *Catalogus Bibliothecae Harvardian Cantabrigiae Nov-Anglorum* (Boston: Fleet, 1790), p. 8.   EAI: E22559; W138

New York, N.Y., Society Library
   Campbell's Vitruvius Britanicus. 3 vols. Folio. ¶ *A catalogue of the books belonging to the New-York Society Library* (New York: Gaine, [1758]), p. 4.
                                    EAI: E8217; W31

Philadelphia, Pa., Library Company
   Vitruvius Britannicus; or, The British Architect: Containing the Plans, Elevations and Sections of the regular Buildings, both publick and private, in Great- Britain. With Variety of new Designs in 200 large Folio Plates, engraven by the best Hands. 2 vols. To which is added

the Geometrical Plans of the most considerable Gardens and Plantations; with large Views in Perspective of the most remarkable Edifices in Great-Britain, engraven by the best Hands in 100 large Folio Plates. By Colin Campbell, Esq; Architect to His Royal Highness the Prince of Wales. London, 1731. Folio. ¶ *Catalogue* (1741), p. 14.

8. *The carpenters rules of work in the town of Boston.* Boston, 1774. (17.5cm)

   Blake, William Pynson (1769-1820), & Lemuel (1775-1861), booksellers, Boston, Mass.
   Carpenter's Rules of Work in the Town of Boston. ¶*Catalogue of books, for sale or circulation, by W. P. & L. Blake* (Boston, 1798), p. 55.   EAI: E33428; W248

9. Castell, Robert (d. 1729). *The villas of the ancients illustrated.* London, 1728. (52cm)   Park 6

   Philadelphia, Pa., Library Company
   The Villas of the Ancients, illustrated, by Robert Cashell. London, 1728. Folio. ¶ *The charter, laws, and catalogue of books, of the Library Company of Philadelphia* (Philadelphia: Franklin & Hall, 1757), p. 25.
   EAI: E8006; W29

10. Chambers, Sir William (1723-96). *Designs of Chinese buildings, furniture, dresses, machines, and utensils. Engraved by the best hands from the originals drawn in China by Mr. Chambers, . . . To which is annexed, a description of their temples, houses, gardens, &c.* London, 1757. (56.5cm)

Charleston, S.C., Library Society
    Chambers's designs. London, 1757. Folio. ¶ *Catalogue* (1770), p. 4. Identified as *Designs of Chinese buildings* by publication date and folio format.

11. Chambers, Sir William (1723-96). *A treatise on civil architecture, in which the principles of that art are laid down, and illustrated by a great number of plates, accurately designed, and elegantly engraved by the best hands.* London, 1759. (51.5cm)   Park 7

    Baltimore, Md., Library Company
       Chambers's Civil Architecture. Folio. ¶ *A catalogue of the books, &c. belonging to the Library Company of Baltimore* (Baltimore: Hayes, 1798), p. 48.
    EAI: E48345; W253

    Harvard College Library, Cambridge, Mass.
       Chambers (Sir Wm.) Treatise on civil architecture. London, 1759. Folio. ¶ *Catalogue* (1790), p. 8.

12. Coggeshall, Henry (1623-1690). *The art of practical measuring, by the sliding rule, shewing, how to measure round, square or other timber, stone, board . . . Also gauging; with instructions in decimals, Mr. Townley's method of logarithms, and the use of the diagonal scale applied to Gunter's chain. By Henry Coggeshall . . . Whereto is added . . . the use of Scamozzi's lines, for finding the lengths and angles of hips, rafters, &c. . . . by John Ham. And to render the book more compleat, in this edition is added, A compendium of practical geometry and the principles of plain trigonometry, with the application thereof, by G. Thomson.* 5th ed. London, 1732. (15cm)

Earlier editions under the titles: *Timber-measure... by a double rule.* London, 1677; *A treatise of measures by a two-foot rule, which slides to a foot.* London, 1682; and *The art of practical measuring easily perform'd, by a two-foot rule, which slides to a foot; on which is the best measure of round timber the common way.* London, 1722. (16cm)

Rivington, James (1724-1802), bookseller, New York, N.Y., & Philadelphia, Pa.
>The Art of Measuring by the sliding Rule, shewing how to Measure round, Square or other Timber, Stone, Glass, Paving, Painting, Wainscot; also, Gauging, with the Use of Scamozzi's Lines, for finding Lengths and Angles of Hips, Rafters, &c. at any pitch, in Square, Bevelling or Tapering Frames; and to render the Book more compleat, is added, a Compendium of practical Geometry, the Principles of plain Trigonometry, with the Application thereof. By G. Thomson. ¶ *Catalogue* (1760), p. 56.

Rivington, James (1724-1802), & Samuel Brown (fl. 1755-69), booksellers, New York, N.Y., & Philadelphia, Pa.
>The Art of Measuring by the sliding Rule, by G. Thomson. ¶ *Catalogue* (1762), p. 52.

13. Columbani, Placido (b. ca.1744). *A new book of ornaments containing a variety of elegant designs for modern pannels. Commonly executed in stucco, wood, or painting, and used in decorating principal rooms.* London, 1775. (35cm)

Bradford, Thomas (1745-1838), bookseller, Philadelphia, Pa.

Coimbani's Books of ornaments. ¶ *Bradford's catalogue of books and stationery, wholesale & retail, for 1796* (Philadelphia: Bradford, 1796), p. 56.
EAI: E30121; W212

Fenno, John Ward (1778-1802), bookseller, New York, N.Y.
Columbani's Ornaments, containing a variety of elegant designs for modern Pannels, 32 plates. ¶ *Supplementary catalogue, consisting of books, imported from London, per the latest arrivals. . . . October, 1800* (New York: Furman, [1800]), p. 5.
EAI: E38098; W279

Nancrede, Paul Joseph Guérard de (1760-1841), bookseller, Boston, Mass.
Columbani's Book of Ornaments. Quarto. ¶ *Books: —importation of May, 1798. Joseph Nancrede's catalogue of books, just imported from London* (Boston, June, 1798), p. 10.
EAI: E34165; W255

Thomas, Isaiah (1749-1831), Ebenezer Turrell Andrews (1766-1851), & Obadiah Penniman (1776-1820), booksellers, Albany, N.Y.
Columbanis' New Book of Ornaments. ¶ *Catalogue of books for sale* (Albany: Andrews, [1797?]), p. 34.
EAI: E32918; W244

14. Columbani, Placido (b. ca.1744). *Variety of capitals, freezes, and corniches, and how to increase, or decrease them, still retaining the same proportion as the original: likewise 12 designs for chimney pieces, drawn an inch and a half to a foot, the whole consisting of 12 plates, published according to*

act of parliament in the year 1776 by P. Columbani. London, [1776]. (25.5 x 34.5cm)

Bradford, Thomas (1745-1838), bookseller, Philadelphia, Pa.
> Coimbani's capital frizes. ¶ *Catalogue* (1796), p. 56.

Fenno, John Ward (1778-1802), bookseller, New York, N.Y.
> A variety of Capitols, Friezes, and Cornishes, and how to increase or decrease them—likewise 12 designs for Chimney-pieces, 12 plates. ¶ *Catalogue* (1800), p. 5.

15. [Crunden, John (ca.1745-1835)]. *The carpenter's companion for Chinese railing and gates. Containing thirty-three entire new and beautiful designs, very proper to be executed at the entrance or round. Chinese temples, summer houses, rotundo, alcove, and umbrelloed seats, parks, grottos, hermitages, ice-houses, islands, cascades, ha! ha's! gardens, courts, yards, &c. Being a work of universal use to carpenters, joyners, &c. and intended to furnish the nobility and gentry with variety of choice. The whole correctly and neatly engraved on sixteen copper plates, from the original drawings of J. H. Morris, carpenter, and J. Crunden.* London, 1765. (22cm)   Park 9

Another edition published under the title: *The carpenter's companion: containing thirty-three designs for all sorts of Chinese railing and gates, engraved on sixteen plates.* London, [n.d.]. (22.5cm)

White, James (1755?-1824), bookseller, Boston, Mass.

Carpenters Companion for Chinese railings, &c. ¶ *A catalogue of books . . . for sale, wholesale or retail, at James White's book and stationary-store* (Boston, [1797?]), p. 8.   EAI: E33215; W247

16. Crunden, John (ca.1745-1835). *Convenient and ornamental architecture, consisting of original designs, for plans, elevations, and sections: beginning with the farmhouse, and regularly ascending to the most grand and magnificent villa; calculated both for town and country, and to suit all persons in every station of life. With a reference and explanation, in letter-press, of the use of every room in each separate building, and the dimensions accurately figured on the plans, with exact scales for measurement. By John Crunden, architect. The whole elegantly engraved on seventy copper-plates, by Isaac Taylor.* Cover title: *Crunden's designs.* London, 1767. (28cm)   Park 10

Bell, Robert (1731?-84), bookseller, Philadelphia, Pa.
Crunden's Convenient and Ornamental Architecture, consisting of original Designs for Plans, Elevations, and Sections; on seventy Copperplates, from the Farm-house to the most grand and magnificent Villa. Quarto. ¶ *Philadelphia, July 15th 1773. Robert Bell's sale catalogue of a collection of new and old books* ([Philadelphia: Bell, 1773]), p. [48].
EAI: E12670; W83

Fenno, John Ward (1778-1802), bookseller, New York, N.Y.
Convenient and Ornamental Architecture, consisting of Original Designs for plans, elevations and sections, beginning with the Farm-house, and regularly ascend-

ing to the most magnificent Villa; by Jno. Crunden. A new edition, 70 copper-plates. ¶ *Catalogue* (1800), pp. [3]-4.

Larkin, Ebenezer (1767-1813), bookseller, Boston, Mass.
Crunden's Designs. Quarto. ¶ *Catalogue* (1793), p. 45.

Philadelphia, Pa., Library Company
Crunden's convenient and ornamental architecture, consisting of original designs for plans, elevations, and sections. With plates. London, 1791. Quarto. ¶ *Second supplement to the catalogue of books, belonging to the Library Company of Philadelphia* (Philadelphia: Poulson, 1794), p. 6.   EAI: E27509; W191

Thomas, Isaiah (1749-1831), & Ebenezer Turrell Andrews (1766-1851), booksellers, Boston, Mass.
Crunden's Designs. Quarto. ¶*Catalogue* (1793), p. 45.

White, James (1755?-1824), bookseller, Boston, Mass.
Crunden's Architecture.   ¶ *Catalogue* (1797?), p. 8.

17. Crunden, John (ca. 1745-1835). *The joyner and cabinet-maker's darling, or pocket director. Containing, sixty different designs, entirely new and useful, forty of which are Gothic, Chinese, mosaic and ornamental frets, proper for friezes, imposts, architraves, tabernacle frames, book-cases, tea tables, tea stands, trays, stoves, and fenders. And twenty new and beautiful designs for Gothic, modern and ornamental fan-lights for over-doors, in the most elegant taste. Calculated for the universal use of carpenters, joyners, cabinet-makers,*

masons, plaisterers, smiths, &c. &c. And intended to assist the nobility and gentry in their choice. The whole designed and engraved by John Crunden, architect. London, 1765. (26cm) Park 11

Larkin, Ebenezer (1767-1813), bookseller, Boston, Mass.
    Joiner and Cabinet Maker's Darling. Octavo. ¶ *Catalogue* (1793), p. 46.

Thomas, Isaiah (1749-1831), & Ebenezer Turrell Andrews (1766-1851), booksellers, Boston, Mass.
    Joiner and Cabinet Maker's Darling. Octavo. ¶ *Catalogue* (1793), p. 46.

Thomas, Isaiah (1749-1831), Ebenezer Turrell Andrews (1766-1851), & Obadiah Penniman (1776-1820), booksellers, Albany, N.Y.
    Joiner and Cabinet-Maker's Darling. ¶ *Catalogue* (1797?), p. 34.

West, David (1765-1810), bookseller, Boston, Mass.
    Joiner and Cabinet Maker's Darling. Octavo. ¶ *David West's catalogue of books, for sale* (Boston: [Thomas & Andrews, 1793]), p. 46.
                                    EAI: E26468; W182

18. Darly, Matthias. *A compleat body of architecture: wherein the five orders are exactly described in many elegant examples, with scales annexed, giving their true aliquot parts. Embellished with a great variety of ornaments adapted thereto; shewing, in one view, the most celebrated decorations used by the ancients, and those which are most approved in the modern taste. Augmented by several new designs, never*

before published. Drawn by the greatest masters, and engraved at an unspared expence, on one hundred and two folio copper plates. Consisting of 1. The five orders, with general proportions. 2. Parts, as entablatures, capitals, bases, &c. on a large scale. 3. Mouldings, with their form and proportions, plain and ornamented. 4. The five orders adapted to doors, gates, intercolumniations, &c. 5. Windows, pediments, ballusters, &c. 6. Cielings, pannels, &c. 7. Chimney pieces, vases, &c. 8. Sections, alcoves, &c. 9. Spandrells, brackets, &c. 10. Frames, masks, rosets, &c. . . . Compiled, drawn, and engraved, by Matthias Darly, professor of ornament. London, 1773. (46cm)

Earlier edition published under the title: *The ornamental architect, or young-artists instructor, consisting of the five orders, drawn by aliquot parts, with their embellishments &c. elegantly engrav'd on (102) folio-plates, by various masters. This work is renderd so easy, that most capacitys, by practice and attention, may draw any piece of architecture required with its ornaments the number of ornamental compositions, and the different manner of expressing antique ornaments, makes it the most usefull workmans book extant, and at the same time it may be renderd the most entertaining work of the kind, for the instruction of the ladys, and gentlemen . . . . Publish'd by the author Matthias Darly professor of ornament & engraver.* [London, 1770]. (46cm)

Bradford, Thomas (1745-1838), bookseller, Philadelphia, Pa.
    Darley's architecture. Folio. ¶ *Catalogue* (1796), p. 56.

19. Decker, Paul. *Chinese architecture, civil and ornamental.*

Being a large collection of the most elegant and useful designs of plans and elevations, &c. from the imperial retreat to the smallest ornamental building in China. Likewise their marine subjects. The whole to adorn gardens, parks, woods, canals, &c. Consisting of great variety, among which are the following, viz. royal garden seats, heads and terminations for canals, alcoves, banqueting houses, temples both open and close, adapted for canals and other ways, bridges, summerhouses, repositories, umbrello'd seats, cool retreats, the summer dwelling of a chief bonza or priest, honorary pagaodas, Japaneze and imperial barges of China. Also those for the emperor's women, and principal officers attending on the emperor, pleasure boats, &c. To which are added, Chinese flowers, landscapes, figures, ornaments, &c. The whole neatly engraved on twenty-four copper-plates, from real designs drawn in China, adapted to this climate, by P. Decker, architect. Volume 2: *Chinese architecture. Part the second. Being a large collection of designs of their paling of different kinds, lattice work, &c. for parks, paddocks, terminations for vistos, ha ha's, common fence and garden, paling, both close and open, Chinese stiles, stair-cases, galleries, windows, &c. To which are added, several designs of Chinese vessels, ewers, ganges cups, tureens, garden pots, &c. The whole neatly engraved on twelve copper-plates, from real Chinese designs, improved by P. Decker, architect.* London, 1759. (21.5 x 28cm)   Park 12

Rivington, James (1724-1802), bookseller, New York, N.Y., & Philadelphia, Pa.
    Decker's Collection of useful Designs of Chinese Buildings. ¶ *Catalogue* (1760), p. 46.

20. Desgodets, Antoine Babuty (1653-1728). *Les édifices an-*

tiques de Rome dessinés et measurés très exactement par Antoine Desgodetz architecte. Paris, 1682. (31cm)

The ancient buildings of Rome, accurately measured and delineated by Anthony Desgodetz. Illustrated with one hundred and thirty-seven plates; and explanations in French and English. The plates engraved and the text translated by the late Mr. G. Marshall, architect. 2 vols. London, 1795. (55cm)

Baltimore, Md., Library Company
    Ancient Buildings of Rome. By Desgodetz. Folio. ¶ *Catalogue* (1798), p. 48.

21. *Designs for chimney-pieces, with mouldings & bases at large; on 24 plates.* London, [1793]. (25.5 x 32cm)

Blake, William Pynson (1769-1820), & Lemuel (1775-1861), booksellers, Boston, Mass.
    Designs for Chimney Pieces. ¶ *Catalogue* (1798), p. 14.

Fenno, John Ward (1778-1802), bookseller, New York, N.Y.
    Designs for Chimney-pieces, with mouldings and bases at large, 24 elegant plates. ¶ *Catalogue* (1800), p. 4.

White, James (1755?-1824), bookseller, Boston, Mass.
    Designs for Chimney Pieces. ¶ *Catalogue* (1797?), p. 10.

22. *Designs for shop-fronts and door-cases.* London, [179-?].

(32cm)

White, James (1755?-1824), bookseller, Boston, Mass.
Designs for Shop Fronts. ¶ *Catalogue* (1797?), p. 10. Also listed as *Carpenters designs for shop fronts and door cases*.

23. Espie, Félix François, comte d' (1708-92). *Maniere de rendre toutes sortes d'édifices incombustibles; ou, traité sur la construction des voutes, faites avec des briques & du plâtre, dites voutes plates; & d'un toit de brique, sans charpente, appellé comble briqueté*. Paris, 1754. (8vo)

The manner of securing all sorts of buildings from fire. Or, a treatise upon the construction of arches made with bricks and plaister, called flat-arches, and of a roof without timber called a bricked-roof: with the addition of some letters that have passed between the Count of Espie and Peter Wyche, esq; on this subject. Adorned with two copper-plates serving to illustrate the whole work. Written in French by monsieur le comte d'Espie, . . . and translated by L. Dutens. London, 1755. (22cm)

Hall, David (1714-72), bookseller, Philadelphia, Pa.
Manner of securing buildings from fire. ¶ *Imported in the last vessels from England, and to be sold by David Hall* ([Philadelphia: Hall, 1768?]), broadsheet.
EAI: E41833; W64

Philadelphia, Pa., Library Company
D'Espie's manner of securing all sorts of buildings from fire; with plates. London. Octavo. ¶ *Catalogue* (1789), p. 254.

24. Félibien, André, sieur des Avaux et de Javercy (1619-95). *Des principes de l'architecture, de la sculpture, de la peinture, et des autres arts qui en dependent. Avec un dictionnaire des termes propres à chacun de ces arts.* Paris, 1676. (28cm)

    Clarkson, Matthew (1758-1825), & Ebenezer Hazard (1744-1817), estate administrators, Philadelphia, Pa.
        Architecture, viz. De Felibien. Quarto. Cuts. ¶ *For sale at public vendue, . . . at the dwelling house of Pierre Eugene du Simitiere* (Philadelphia: Cist, [1785]), broadside.   EAI: E18402; W106

25. Ferrerio, Pietro (1600-54), & Giovanni Battista Falda (1648-78). *Palazzi di Roma de piu celebri architetti. Disegnati da Pietro Ferrerio pittore et, architetto.* Volume 2: . . . *Nuovi disegni dell' architetture, e plante dè palazzi di Roma dè più celebri architetti, disegnati, et intagliati da Gio: Battista Falda, dati in Luce da Gio: Giocomo de Rossi in Roma.* 2 vols. in 1. Roma, [1655]-78. (36.5 x 47cm)

                                                    Park 14

    Prichard, William (fl.1782-1809), bookseller, Philadelphia, Pa.
        Palazzi di Roma de più celebri Architetti disegnati Pietro Ferrerio. Folio. ¶ *A catalogue of a scarce and valuable collection of books, which are now selling by William Prichard, bookseller and stationer, at the American Circulating Library* ([Philadelphia, 1785]), p. 3.   EAI: E19205; W107

26. Fréart, Roland, Sieur de Chambray (ca. 1606-76). *Parallele de l'architecture antique et de la moderne, avec un recueil des dix principaux auteurs qui ont écrit des cinq ordres, sçauoir,*

Palladio et Scamozzi, Serlio et Vignola, D. Barbaro et Cataneo, L. B. Alberti et Viola, Bullant et de Lorme, comparez entre'eux. Les trois ordres Grecs, le Dorique, l'Ionique & le Corinthien, sont la premiere partie de ce traitté: et les deux Latins, le Toscan & le Composite, en font la derniere. Paris, 1650. (35cm)

A parallel of the antient architecture with the modern, in a collection of ten principal authors who have written upon the five orders, viz. Palladio and Scamozzi, Serlio and Vignola, D. Barbaro and Cataneo, L. B. Alberti and Viola, Bullant and De Lorme, compared with one another. The three Greek orders, Dorique, Ionique, and Corinthian, comprise the first part of this treatise. And the two Latine, Tuscan and Composita the latter. Written in French by Roland Freart, Sieur de Chambray; made English for the benefit of builders. To which is added an account of architects and architecture, in an historical, and etymological explanation of certain tearms particularly affected by architects. With Leon Baptista Alberti's treatise of statues. By John Evelyn esq. London, 1664. (34cm)   Park 15

Cambell, Duncan (fl. 1693-95), bookseller, Boston, Mass. Evenius parallel of Architecture. ¶ *The library of the late Reverend and Learned Mr. Samuel Lee* [1625-91] (Boston, 1693), p. 9. Identified as Fréart de Chambray's *A parallel of the antient architecture with the modern* by Helen Park, *A List of Architectural Books Available in America Before the Revolution* (Los Angeles, 1973).   EAI: E645; W1

Charleston, S.C., Library Society
    Evelyn's paralell of ancient and modern architecture.

London, 1733. Folio. ¶ *Catalogue* (1770), p. 6.

Moreau de Saint-Méry, Médéric Louis Elie (1750-1819), & Company, booksellers, Philadelphia, Pa.
    Architecture moderne, ou paralelle de l'Architecture antique avec la moderne, suivant les dix principaux auteurs qui ont ecrit sur les cinq ordres par Errard & de Chambray. Octavo. ¶ *Catalogue of books* (Philadelphia: [Moreau de Saint-Méry], 1795), p. 32. EAI: E29107; W205

New York, N.Y., Corporation of the City of New York Library
    Freart's Paralel of Architecture, by Evelyn. London, 1707. Folio. ¶ *A catalogue of the library, belonging to the Corporation of the City of New-York* (New York: Holt, 1766), p. 6.   EAI: 41648; W57

27. Garret, Daniel (d. 1753). *Designs, and estimates, of farm houses, &c. for the county of York, Northumberland, Cumberland, Westmoreland, and bishoprick of Durham.* London, 1747. (42cm)   Park 16

Cox, Edward (fl. 1766-78), & Edward Berry (fl. 1766-72), booksellers, Boston, Mass.
    Garret's Designs for Farm Houses. Octavo. ¶ *A catalogue of a very large assortment of the most esteemed books in every branch of polite literature, arts and sciences* ([Boston, 1772?]), p. 12.   EAI: E42336; W79

Noel, Garrat (fl. 1752-75), bookseller, New York, N.Y.
    Designs and Estimates for building of Farm Houses. ¶ *A catalogue of books* (New York: Gaine, 1762), p.

27.   EAI: E9222; W44

Noel, Garrat (fl. 1752-75), & Ebenezer Hazard (1744-1817), booksellers, New York, N.Y.
> Garret's Designs and Estimates for building Farm Houses. ¶ *A catalogue of books, sold by Noel and Hazard, at their book and stationary store* (New York: Inslee & Car, 1771), p. 18.   EAI: E12168; W76

Rivington, James (1724-1802), & Samuel Brown (fl. 1755-69), booksellers, New York, N.Y., & Philadelphia, Pa.
> Garrett's Designs for Farm Houses, by which a Person may be his own Judge before he begins to build, what sort of a House will best suit the Farm he intends it for without leaving it to unskilful Workmen, calculated to serve any Country. ¶ *Catalogue* (1762), p. 66.

28. Gauger, Nicolas (1680?-1730). *La mecanique du feu, ou l'art d'en augmenter les effects, & d'en diminuer la depénse. Premiere partie, contenant le traité de nouvelles chiminées qui échauffent plus que les chiminées ordinaires, & qui ne sont point sujettes à fumer, &c. Par Mr G****. Paris, 1713. (15.5cm)

Fires improv'd: being a new method of building chimneys, so as to prevent their smoking: in which a small fire, shall warm a room better than a much larger made the common way. With the manner of altering such chimneys as are already built, so that they shall perform the same effects. Illustrated with cuts. Written in French, by Monsieur Gauger: made English and improved, by J.[ohn] T.[heophilus]

Architectural Books in Early America

Desaguliers, M.A.F.R.S. By whom is added, the manner of making coal-fires, as useful this new-way, as the wood-fires propos'd by the French author, explain'd by an additional plate. The whole being suited to the capacity of the meanest work-man. London, 1715. (16cm)

Newport, R.I., Redwood Library
Fires improved, by Desaguliers. Duodecimo. ¶ *Catalogue* (1764), p. 18.

New York, N.Y., Society Library
Desagular's Gaugers Fires, improv'd. Octavo. ¶ *Catalogue* (1758), p. 11.

Philadelphia, Pa., Library Company
Fires improved; or, A new Method of building Chimnies, so as to prevent their Smoaking. In which a small Fire shall warm a Room much better than a large one made the common Way. By Mons. Gauger. Made English from the French Original, by J. T. Desaguliers, LL.D. and F.R.S. 2d Edit. with an Appendix containing several farther Improvements. London, 1736. Octavo. (Gift of Mr. Grace) ¶ *Catalogue* (1741), p. 37.

Philadelphia, Pa., Loganian Library
Guager, la Mechanique du Feu, ou un Traité de nouvelles Chiminées qui echauffent plue que les ordinaires, et qui ne sont pas sujettes a fumer. Amsterdam, 1714. Octavo. ¶*Catalogus Bibliothecae Loganiane* (Philadelphia: Miller, 1760), p. 103.

EAI: E8715; W40

Rhode Island College Library [Brown University], Providence, R.I.
> Gauger on smoking Chimnies. Duodecimo. ¶ *Catalogue of books belonging to the Library of Rhode-Island College* (Providence: Carter, 1793), p. 30.
> EAI: E26077; W180

29. Gibbs, James (1682-1754). *A book of architecture, containing designs of buildings and ornaments.* London, 1728. (49cm)   Park 17

> Charleston, S.C., Library Society
> > Gibbes's architecture. London, 1739. Folio. ¶ *Catalogue* (1770), p. 6.
>
> Guild, Benjamin (1749-92), bookseller, Boston, Mass.
> > Gibbs on Architecture. Folio. ¶ *Catalogue* (1787?; E22545), p. 11. Advertised for sale again in 1789.
>
> Hall, David (1714-72), bookseller, Philadelphia, Pa.
> > Gibb's architecture. ¶ *Imported in the last vessels from Europe* ([Philadelphia: Franklin & Hall, 1763?]), broadsheet. Advertised for sale again in 1767 and 1768.   EAI: E41386; W48
>
> Knox, Henry (1750-1806), bookseller, Boston, Mass.
> > Gibb's beautiful designs for churches. Folio. ¶ *A Catalogue of books, imported and to be sold by Henry Knox* ([Boston, 1773]), p. 18.   EAI: E12424; W87
>
> New York, N.Y., Society Library
> > Gibb's (James) architecture, containing designs of buildings and ornaments. Folio. ¶ *The charter, bye-*

laws, ... With a catalogue of the books (New York: Gaine, 1789), p. 35.   EAI: E22018; W133

Philadelphia, Pa., Library Company
　Gibbs (James) his Book of Architecture: containing Designs of Buildings and Ornaments. 2d ed. London, 1739. Folio. ¶ Catalogue (1775), p. 26.

Rivington, James (1724-1802), bookseller, New York, N.Y., & Philadelphia, Pa.
　Gibb's Architecture. ¶ Catalogue (1760), p. 45.

Rivington, James (1724-1802), & Samuel Brown (fl. 1755-69), booksellers, New York, N.Y., & Philadelphia, Pa.
　Gibbs's Architecture. ¶ Catalogue (1762), p. 66.

30. Gibbs, James (1682-1754). *Rules for drawing the several parts of architecture, in a more exact and easy manner than has been heretofore practised, by which all fractions, in dividing the principal members and their parts, are avoided.* London, 1732. (47cm)　　　　　　　　　Park 18

Bradford, Thomas (1745-1838), bookseller, Philadelphia, Pa.
　Gibb's rules for drawing. ¶ Catalogue (1796), p. 56.

Charleston, S.C., Library Society
　Gibbes's rules of drawing, particularly regarding architecture. London, 1738. Folio. ¶ Catalogue (1770), p. 6.

Hall, David (1714-72), bookseller, Philadelphia, Pa.

Gibb's Rules for Drawing. Folio. ¶ *Catalogue* (1754), broadside. Advertised for sale again in 1760 and 1761.

New York, N.Y., Society Library
Gibb's (James) rules for drawing the several parts of architecture. Folio. ¶ *Catalogue* (1789), p. 35.

Philadelphia, Pa., Library Company
Gibb's (James) Rules for drawing the several Parts of Architecture, in a more exact and easy manner, than has been heretofore practis'd; by which all fractions in dividing the principal members, and their parts, are avoided. 3rd ed. London, 1753. Folio. ¶ *The charter, laws, and catalogue of books, of the Library Company of Philadelphia* (Philadelphia: Crukshank, 1770), n.p.   EAI: E11820; W74

Rivington, James (1724-1802), bookseller, New York, N.Y., & Philadelphia, Pa.
Gibb's Rules for Drawing. ¶ *Catalogue* (1760), p. 45.

Rivington, James (1724-1802), & Samuel Brown (fl. 1755-69), booksellers, New York, N.Y., & Philadelphia, Pa.
Gibbs's Rules for Drawing. ¶ *Catalogue* (1762), p. 66.

31. Good, John. *Measuring made easy; or, the description and use of Coggeshall's sliding rule, containing instructions for measuring all manner of timber, both by the common way, and the true way: with directions for taking the dimensions of trees, and the allowance for bark, &c. performed both by the rule, and by arithmetick; by which may be measured all manner of superfices, as board, glass, plaistering, painting,*

wainscotting, tyleing, paving, land, &c. both by the rule and arithmetick. By J. Good, teacher of mathematicks. Carefully corrected and much enlarged by J. Atkinson, sen. London, 1719. (15cm)

Campbell, Samuel (1763?-1836), bookseller, New York, N.Y.
> Good's measurer. Edinburgh, 1775. Octavo. ¶ *Samuel Campbell's sale catalogue of books, for 1794* ([New York: S. Campbell, 1794]), p. 33.
>
> EAI: E26728; W184

32. Halfpenny, William (d. 1755). *The art of sound building; demonstrated in geometrical problems: shewing geometrical lines for all kinds of arches, niches, groins, and twisted rails, both regular and irregular. With several other draughts of buildings and staircases. All curiously engraven on copper plates. Wherein are laid down (suited to every capacity) easy practical methods for carpenters, joiners, masons, or bricklayers, to work by.* London, 1725. (30.5cm)   Park 19

Bradford, Thomas (1745-1838), bookseller, Philadelphia, Pa.
> Halfpenny's geometrical architecture. ¶ *Catalogue* (1796), p. 56. Identified as Halfpenny's *The art of sound building* by Philip M. Johnston, 'A Checklist of Books Relating to Architecture and the Decorative Arts Available in Philadelphia in the Three Decades Following 1780.' (M.A. thesis, University of Delaware, 1974).

33. [Halfpenny, William (d. 1755)]. *The builder's pocket-companion. Shewing an easy and practical method for laying*

down of lines, for all sorts of arches and curves used in house-building, ship-building, gardening, &c. also to make the centers or ribs for vaults or cielings, and brackets for coves, either regular or irregular. Together with true and concise rules to find the lengths, bevels, and moulds for the back of a hip, in any kind of roofs, whether square or bevel, hexagon or pentagon, &c. let their rafters be straight, or curves of different sorts. Extracted from the works of several noted authors: illustrated with variety of examples curiously engraven; and several useful problems added never before printed; by Michael Hoare [pseud.], carpenter. London, 1728. (17cm)   Park 20

Hall, David (1714-72), bookseller, Philadelphia, Pa.
    Builder's pocket companion. ¶ *Imported in the last vessels from England* ([Philadelphia: Hall, 1767]), p. [1]. Advertised for sale again in 1768 and 1769.
                                                  EAI: E41719; W62

34. Halfpenny, William (d. 1755), and John Halfpenny (fl. 1750). *Chinese and Gothic architecture properly ornamented. Being twenty new plans and elevations, on twelve copper-plates: containing a great variety of magnificent buildings accurately described; as also, several of a smaller kind elegantly design'd, with all necessary offices, of great strength, easy construction, and graceful appearance. Scales are annexed, and regular estimates are made for each design. The whole carefully calculated by the great square; with instructions to workmen, &c. in several pages of letter-press. Intended as an improvement of what has been published of that sort. Correctly engraved from the designs of William and John Halfpenny, architects.* London, 1752. (28cm)

Noel, Garrat (fl. 1752-75), bookseller, New York, N.Y.
   Halfpenny's, Chinese and Gothic Architecture. ¶ *Catalogue* (1762), p. 27.

35. Halfpenny, William (d.1755), & John Halfpenny (fl.1750). *The country gentleman's pocket companion, and builder's assistant, for rural decorative architecture. Containing thirty-two new designs, plans and elevations of alcoves, floats, temples, summer-houses, lodges, huts, grotto's, &c., in the Augustine, Gothick and Chinese taste, with proper directions annexed. Also, an exact estimate of their several amounts, which are from twenty-five to one hundred pounds, and most of them portable. Correctly engraved on twenty-five copper plates, from the designs, . . . of William and John Halfpenny, architects.* London, 1753. (20.5cm)   Park 21

Noel, Garrat (fl. 1752-75), & Ebenezer Hazard (1744-1817), booksellers, New York, N.Y.
   Halfpenny's Gentleman's Assistant in Building. ¶ *Catalogue* (1771), p. 18.

Rivington, James (1724-1802), bookseller, New York, N.Y., & Philadelphia, Pa.
   Halfpenny's Country Gentleman's and Builder's Pocket Companion, containing Designs, &c. for Lodges, Huts, Summer-Houses, Grottos, &c. ¶ *Catalogue* (1760), p. 46.

Rivington, James (1724-1802), & Samuel Brown (fl. 1755-69), booksellers, New York, N.Y., & Philadelphia, Pa.
   Halfpenny's Country Gentleman's and Builder's Pocket Companion, containing Designs, &c. for

Lodges, Huts, Summer-Houses, Grottos, &c. ¶ *Catalogue* (1762), p. 67.

36. Halfpenny, William (d. 1755), John Halfpenny (fl. 1750), Robert Morris (ca. 1702-54), and Thomas Lightoler. *The modern builder's assistant; or, a concise epitome of the whole system of architecture; in which the various branches of that excellent study are establish'd on the most familiar principles, and rendered adequate to every capacity; being useful to the proficient, and easy to the learner. Divided into three parts. Containing I. A correct view of the five orders, explained in several sheets of letter-press. II. Consisting of regular plans, elevations, and sections of houses, in the most elegant and convenient manner, either for the reception of noblemen, gentlemen or tradesmen with large or small families, adapted to the taste of town or country. To which part is added, a great variety of other plans for offices or out-houses adjoining to them of different dimensions for domestic uses; such as kitchens, wash-houses, malt-houses, bake-houses, brew-houses, dairies, vaults, stables, coach-houses, dog-kennels, &c. &c. Together with the estimates of each design, and proper instructions to the workmen how to execute the same. III. Exhibiting (ornamental as well as plain) a variety of chimney-pieces, windows, doors, sections of stair-cases, rooms, halls, saloons, &c. skreens for rooms, also cieling, piers, and gate-roofs, &c. &c. The whole beautifully engraved on eighty five folio copper plates, from the designs of William and John Halfpenny, architects and carpenters, Robert Morris, surveyor, and T. Lightoler, carver.* London, 1742. (31cm)

Park 22

Bell, Robert (1731?-84), bookseller, Philadelphia, Pa.
The Modern Builders Assistant, or, a Concise

Epitome of the whole System of Architecture, containing eighty beautiful folio Copperplates, by Halfpenny, Morris and Lightoler. Folio. ¶ *Catalogue* (1773), p. 4.

Bradford, Thomas (1745-1838), bookseller, Philadelphia, Pa.
Halfpenny's modern builder. ¶ *Catalogue* (1796), p. 56.

Hall, David (1714-72), bookseller, Philadelphia, Pa.
Modern Builder's Assistant. Folio. ¶ *Books imported in the last vessel from London* ([Philadelphia: Franklin & Hall, 1760?]), broadside.   EAI: E8362; W38

Noel, Garrat (fl. 1752-75), bookseller, New York, N.Y.
Modern Builder. ¶ *A catalogue of books, . . . to be sold, by Garrat Noel, and Company* (New York: Gaine, 1759), p. 17.   EAI: E8447; W33

Rivington, James (1724-1802), bookseller, New York, N.Y., & Philadelphia, Pa.
The Modern Builder's Assistant, or a concise Epitome of the whole System of Architecture, by Halfpenny, Morris, &c. ¶ *Catalogue* (1760), p. 46.

Rivington, James (1724-1802), & Samuel Brown (fl. 1755-69), booksellers, New York, N.Y., & Philadelphia, Pa.
The Modern Builder's Assistant, or a concise Epitome of the whole System of Architecture, by Halfpenny, Morris, &c. ¶ *Catalogue* (1762), p. 67.

37. Halfpenny, William (d. 1755). *A new and compleat system of architecture delineated, in a variety of plans and elevations of designs for convenient and decorated houses. Together with offices and out-buildings proportioned thereto, and appropriated to the several uses and situations required. As also an estimate of each by the great square. Prefix'd to these are ten different sorts of piers, with gates of various compositions suitable to the same; intended for entrances to courts, gardens, &c. As also new architectonic rules for drawing the members, in all kinds and proportions of the orders. And to them are also added a perspective view of the sinking pier of Westminster-bridge, with the two adjoining arches; and a method proposed by trusses &c. to take off ¾ of the weight, or abutment and pressure now on the pier, and discharge it as set forth on the plate. The whole comprised on 47 copper plates, with explanations thereto in common press-work. Neatly engraved, and design'd by William Half-penny, architect.* London, 1749. (21.5 x 26.5cm) Park 23

Blake, William Pynson (1769-1820), bookseller, Boston, Mass.
    Halfpenny's new and complete system of Architecture. ¶ *A catalogue of books, for sale or circulation, by William P. Blake* (Boston, 1793), p. 20.
        EAI: E25206; W168

Boston, Mass., broadside, September 30, 1766
    Halfpenny's System. ¶ *Boston, September 30, 1766. On Monday, the 13th of October next, will be offered to sale at a store in Union-Street, . . . a valuable collection of books* ([Boston, 1766]), broadside.
        EAI: E41605; W56

Bradford, Thomas (1745-1838), bookseller, Philadelphia, Pa.
 Halfpenny's complete system of architecture. ¶ *Catalogue* (1796), p. 56.

Guild, Benjamin (1749-92), bookseller, Boston, Mass.
 Halfpenny's new and complete System of Architecture. Quarto. ¶ *Addition to a catalogue of a large assortment of books* ([Boston, 1787?]), p. 9. Advertised for sale again in 1789.   EAI: E45266; W118

Knox, Henry (1750-1806), bookseller, Boston, Mass.
 Halfpenny's Architecture delineated. ¶ *Catalogue* (1773), p. 19.

Noel, Garrat (fl. 1752-75), bookseller, New York, N.Y.
 Halfpenny's System of Architecture. ¶ *Catalogue* (1762), p. 27.

Noel, Garrat (fl. 1752-75), & Ebenezer Hazard (1744-1817), booksellers, New York, N.Y.
 Halfpenny's new and complete System of Architecture. ¶ *Catalogue* (1771), p. 18.

Rivington, James (1724-1802), & Samuel Brown (fl. 1755-69), booksellers, New York, N.Y., & Philadelphia, Pa.
 Halfpenny's new and complete System of Architecture. ¶ *Catalogue* (1762), p. 66.

38. Halfpenny, William (d. 1755). *Practical architecture, or a sure guide to the true working according to the rules of that science: representing the five orders, with their several doors*

Architectural Books in Early America

& windows, taken from Inigo Jones & other celebrated architects; to each plate tables containing the exact proportions of the several parts are likewise fitted. Very useful to all true lovers of architecture, but particularly so to those who are engag'd in ye noble art of building by Willm. Halfpenny. London, 1724. (17cm) Park 26

Bradford, Thomas (1745-1838), bookseller, Philadelphia, Pa.
   Halfpenny's practical architecture. ¶ *Catalogue* (1796), p. 56.

Dunlap, William (d. 1779), bookseller, Philadelphia, Pa.
   Practical Architecture. ¶ *Books and stationary, just imported from London, and to be sold by W. Dunlap* ([Philadelphia: Dunlap, 1760]), n.p.
                              EAI: E8587; W37

Hall, David (1714-72), bookseller, Philadelphia, Pa.
   Halfpenny's architecture. Duodecimo. ¶ *Catalogue* (1760?), broadside. Advertised for sale again in 1761, 1767, 1768, and 1769. Identified as Halfpenny's *Practical architecture* by the size of the volume.

39. Halfpenny, William (d. 1755), & John Halfpenny (fl. 1750). *Rural architecture in the Chinese taste, being designs entirely new for the decoration of gardens, parks, forrests, insides of houses, &c. on sixty copper plates with full instructions for workmen also a near estimate of the charge, and hints where proper to be erected. The whole invented & drawn by Willm & Jno Halfpenny, architects. Divided into four parts.* 2d ed. London, 1752. (22cm)

Originally issued in four parts under the titles: Part I. *New designs for Chinese temples, triumphal arches, garden seats, palings &c. on fourteen copper plates by William Halfpenny architect.* London, 1750. Part II. *New designs for Chinese bridges, temples, triumphal arches, garden seats, palings, obelisks, termini's, &c. on fourteen copper plates. Together with full instructions to workmen annex'd to each particular design; a near estimate of their charge, and hints where with most advantage to be erected. The whole invented and drawn by Will. and John Halfpenny, architects.* London, 1751. Part III. *New designs for Chinese doors, windows, piers, pilasters, garden seats, green houses, summer houses, &c. on sixteen copper plates. Together with instructions to workmen, annex'd to each particular design; the whole invented and drawn by Will. and John Halfpenny, architects.* London, 1751. Part IV. *New designs for Chinese gates, palisades, stair-cases, chimney-pieces, cielings, garden-seats, chairs, temples, &c. on sixteen copper-plates, with full instructions to workmen.* London, 1752. (20cm)

Bradford, Thomas (1745-1838), bookseller, Philadelphia, Pa.
    Halfpenny's rural architecture in the chinese taste. ¶ *Catalogue* (1796), p. 56.

40. Halfpenny, William (d. 1755), and John Halfpenny (fl. 1750). *Rural architecture in the Gothic taste. Being twenty new designs, for temples, garden-seats, summer-houses, lodges, terminies, piers, &c. on sixteen copper plates. With instructions to workmen, and hints where with most advantage to be erected. The whole invented and drawn by William and John Halfpenny, architects.* London, 1752. (20cm)

    Park 27

Architectural Books in Early America

Bradford, Thomas (1745-1838), bookseller, Philadelphia, Pa.
    Halfpenny's rural architecture. ¶ *Catalogue* (1796), p. 56. Identified as Halfpenny's *Rural architecture in the Gothic taste* by Johnston, probably because Bradford had a separate entry for Halfpenny's *Rural architecture in the Chinese taste.*

Rivington, James (1724-1802), bookseller, New York, N.Y., & Philadelphia, Pa.
    Halfpenny's Rural Architecture, in the Gothic Taste. ¶ *Catalogue* (1760), p. 46.

41. Halfpenny, William (d. 1755). *Twelve beautiful designs for farm-houses, with their proper offices and estimates of the whole and every distinct building separate; with the measurement, and value of each particular article, adapted to the customary measurements of most part of England, but more particularly for the following counties, viz. Middlesex, Surry, Essex, Kent, Sussex, Hampshire, Hertfordshire, Cambridgeshire, Berkshire, Buckinghamshire, Oxfordshire, Wiltshire, Gloucestershire, Somersetshire, &c. Useful for gentlemen, builders, &c.* London, 1750. (26cm)   Park 28

Cox, Edward (fl. 1766-78), & Edward Berry (fl. 1766-72), booksellers, Boston, Mass.
    Halfpenny's Farm Houses. Quarto. ¶ *Catalogue* (1772?), p. 13.

Rivington, James (1724-1802), & Samuel Brown (fl. 1755-69), booksellers, New York, N.Y., & Philadelphia, Pa.
    Halfpenny's 12 beautiful Designs for Farm Houses.

¶ *Catalogue* (1762), p. 66.

42. Halfpenny, William (d. 1755). *Twenty new designs of Chinese lattice and other works for stair-cases, gates, palings, hatches, &c on six folio copper plates.* London, 1750. (28cm)
Park 29

Rivington, James (1724-1802), bookseller, New York, N.Y., & Philadelphia, Pa.
Halfpenny's Chinese Latices and Palings. ¶ *Catalogue* (1760), p. 46.

43. Halfpenny, William (d. 1755). *Useful architecture in twenty-one new designs for erecting parsonage-houses, farm-houses, and inns; with their respective offices, &c. of various dimensions at the most moderate expence, the largest not exceeding five hundred pounds, and the smallest under one hundred pounds. As will evidently appear by their several dimensions and estimates, particularly set forth with respect both to brick and stone, adapted to the usual measurement of Great Britain and Ireland. Together with a supplement, containing several designs for building with timber only, with estimates annext in like manner.* London, 1752. (19.5cm)
Park 30

Albany, N.Y., Albany Library
Halfpenny's useful Architecture. Octavo. ¶ *A catalogue of the books belonging to the Albany Library* (Albany: Barber & Southwick, 1793), p. 25.
EAI: E46680; W167

Bradford, Thomas (1745-1838), bookseller, Philadelphia, Pa.

Halfpenny's useful architecture. ¶ *Catalogue* (1796), p. 56.

New York, N.Y., Society Library
Halfpenny's useful Architecture. Octavo. ¶ *Catalogue* (1758), p. 12.

Noel, Garrat (fl. 1752-75), bookseller, New York, N.Y.
Halfpenny's useful Architecture. ¶ *Catalogue* (1762), p. 27.

Noel, Garrat (fl. 1752-75), & Ebenezer Hazard (1744-1817), booksellers, New York, N.Y.
Halfpenny's useful Architecture. ¶ *Catalogue* (1771), p. 18.

Philadelphia, Pa., Library Company
Useful Architecture, in Twenty-one new Designs, for erecting Parsonage Houses, Farm-Houses and Inns, with their respective Offices, &c. of various Dimensions, at the most moderate Expence, the largest not exceeding Five Hundred Pounds, and the smallest under One Hundred Pounds, as will evidently appear by their several Dimensions and Estimates particularly set forth, with respect to both Brick and Stone; adapted to the usual Measurement of Great Britain and Ireland: Together with a Supplement, containing several Designs for building with Timber only; with Estimates annexed in like Manner. By William Halfpenny, Architect and Carpenter. 1752. Octavo. ¶ *Catalogue* (1757), pp. 97-98.

Rivington, James (1724-1802), bookseller, New York, N.Y., & Philadelphia, Pa.

Halfpenny's Useful Architecture, consisting of Designs and full Instruction for erecting Farm-Houses, Inns, Parsonage-Houses, &c. with their several Offices, &c. of various Dimensions, the highest Expence of Building which not exceeding £.500, and the smallest under £.100. ¶ *Catalogue* (1760), p. 46.

Rivington, James (1724-1802), & Samuel Brown (fl. 1755-69), booksellers, New York, N.Y., & Philadelphia, Pa.

Halfpenny's Useful Architecture, consisting of Designs and full Instruction for erecting Farm Houses, Inns, Parsonage-Houses, &c. with their several Offices, &c. of various Dimensions, the highest Expence of Building which not exceeding £.500, and the smallest under £.100. ¶ *Catalogue* (1762), p. 67.

44. Hawney, William. *The compleat measurer; or, the whole art of measuring. In two parts. The first part teaching decimal arithmetick, with the extraction of the square and cube roots. And also the multiplication of feet and inches, commonly call'd cross-multiplication. The second part teaching to measure all sorts of superfices and solids, by decimals, by cross-multiplication, and by scale and compasses. Also the works of several artificers relating to building; and the measuring of board and timber: shewing the common errors. And some practical questions.* London, 1717. (17cm)

Park 106

Allen, Thomas (fl. 1785-99), bookseller, New York, N.Y.
Hawney's Complete Measurer. Duodecimo. ¶ *Thomas Allen's sale catalogue of books* (New York, 1792), p. 24. EAI: E24033; W153

Bradford, Thomas (1745-1838), bookseller, Philadelphia, Pa.
Hawney's complete measurer. Duodecimo. ¶ *Catalogue* (1796), p. 42.

Bradford, William (1719-91), & Thomas (1745-1838), booksellers, Philadelphia, Pa.
Hawney's Measurer. ¶ *William and Thomas Bradford, . . . have for sale, the following books and stationary* ([Philadelphia: W. & T. Bradford, 1767?]), broadside. EAI: E41699; W61

Campbell, Robert (d. 1800), bookseller, New York, N.Y.
Hawney's Complete Measurer. ¶ *A [ca]talo[g]u[e] of [b]oo[k]s, sold by Robert Campbell* ([Philadelphia, 1790?]), broadside. Advertised for sale again in 1791, 1794, and 1796. EAI: E22388; W136

Carey, Mathew (1760-1839), bookseller, Philadelphia, Pa.
Hawney's complete measurer. Duodecimo. ¶ *Catalogue* (1794), p. 51.

Childs, Francis (1763-1830), & Company, booksellers, New York, N.Y.
A Complete Measurer, or the Whole Art of Measuring, &c. by Wm. Hawney. Duodecimo. ¶ *New York, Nov. 1793. Francis Childs & Co's. sale catalogue of books* (New York: Childs & Swaine, 1793), p. 19.

EAI: E25295; W171

Cox, Edward (fl. 1766-78), & Edward Berry (fl. 1766-72), booksellers, Boston, Mass.
    Hawney's Measuring. Duodecimo. ¶ *Catalogue* (1772?), p. 14.

Crukshank, Joseph (1746?-1836), bookseller, Philadelphia, Pa.
    Hawney's Mensuration. ¶ *A catalogue of books to be sold by Joseph Crukshank* ([Philadelphia: Crukshank,] 1789), p. 8.   EAI: E45461; W128

Hall, David (1714-72), bookseller, Philadelphia, Pa.
    Hawney's measurer. ¶ *Catalogue* (1763?), broadsheet. Advertised for sale again in 1767 and possibly as early as 1761 as *Complete Measurer*.

Hall, William (1752-1834), bookseller, Philadelphia, Pa.
    Hawney's Measurer. Duodecimo. ¶ *William Hall, ... has to dispose of, wholesale and retail, the following books, &c.* ([Philadelphia: Hall & Sellers, 1774?], broadsheet.   EAI: E13312; W91

Mein, John (fl. 1760-75), bookseller, Boston, Mass.
    Hawney's Measuring. London, 1765. ¶ *A catalogue of Mein's Circulating Library* ([Boston: [McAlpine & Fleeming], 1765), p. 56. Advertised for sale again in 1766.   EAI: E10069; W54

Noel, Garrat (fl. 1752-75), & Ebenezer Hazard (1744-1817), booksellers, New York, N.Y.
    Hawney's Complete Measurer. ¶ *Catalogue* (1771),

p. 17.

Philadelphia, Pa., Union Library Company
Compleat Measurer; by William Hawney. 5th Edition. Duodecimo. ¶ *A catalogue of books, belonging to the Union Library Company of Philadelphia* (Philadelphia: Miller, 1765), p. 9.
EAI: E10139; W55

Prichard, William (fl. 1782-1809), bookseller, Philadelphia, Pa.
Hawney's Mensuration. ¶ *William Prichard's catalogue of books* ([Philadelphia, 1789]), p. 8.
EAI: E21405; W134

Providence, R.I., Providence Library
Hawney's compleat Measurer. Duodecimo. ¶ *Catalogue of all the books, belonging to the Providence Library* (Providence: Waterman & Russell, 1768), p. 9.
EAI: E11051; W66

Rice, Henry (d. 1804), & Company, booksellers, Philadelphia, Pa.
Hawney's Complete Measurer. Duodecimo. ¶ *Rice and Co. booksellers and stationers, ... have imported in the last vessels from London, Dublin, and Glasgow, a large and general assortment of books* ([Philadelphia, 1789?]), broadside. Advertised for sale again in 1790.
EAI: E45579; W135

Rivington, James (1724-1802), & Samuel Brown (fl. 1755-69), booksellers, New York, N.Y., & Philadelphia, Pa.

Hawney's Practical Measurer. ¶ *Catalogue* (1762), p. 46.

Sparhawk, John (1730-1803), bookseller, Philadelphia, Pa.
Hawney's mensuration. Small octavo or duodecimo. ¶ *A catalogue of books, . . . to be sold by John Sparhawk* ([Philadelphia, 1774?]), p. 33.   EAI: E42507; W92

45. Hodgson, Ph. Levi. *The complete measurer adapted to timber and building, agreeable to the Irish standard . . . with concise and easy method of keeping accounts by day-book and ledger.* 7th ed. Dublin, 1779. (20cm)

Rice, Henry (d. 1804), & Company, booksellers, Philadelphia, Pa.
Hodgson's Measuring.   ¶ *Rice and Co's catalogue of books* ([Philadelphia, 1790?]), p. 41.
EAI: E46274; W144

Rice, Henry (d. 1804), & Patrick (fl. 1792-1804), booksellers, Philadelphia, Pa.
Hodgson's complete measurer. ¶ *Henry and Patrick Rice's catalogue of a large and valuable collection of books . . . for 1795* (Philadelphia, [1795]), p. 70. Advertised for sale again in 1796.
EAI: E47580; W207

Spotswood, William (1753?-1805), bookseller, Boston, Mass., & Philadelphia, Pa.
Hodgson's complete measurer. Adapted to timber and building, with a concise and easy method of keeping accounts by day-book and ledger. 7th ed. ¶ *William Spotswood's catalogue of books* (Boston:

[Spotswood], 1795), p. 59.   EAI: E29558; W208

46. Hoppus, Edward (d. 1739). *The gentleman's and builder's repository: or, architecture display'd. Containing the most useful and requisite problems in geometry. As also, the most easy, expeditious, and correct methods for attaining the knowledge of the five orders of architecture, by equal parts, and fewer divisions, than any thing hitherto published. Together with all such rules for arches, doors, windows cieling-pieces, chimney-pieces, and their particular embellishments, as can be required. Likewise, a large variety of designs for truss roofs; with the method of finding the hip, either square or bevel. Also, the most certain and approved methods of forming a number of different stair-cases, with their twisted rails, &c. The whole embellished, not only with fourscore plates, in quarto, but such variety of cieling-pieces, shields, compartments, and other curious and uncommon decorations, as must needs render it acceptable to all gentlemen, artificers, and others, who delight in, or practice, the art of building. The designs regulated and drawn by E. Hoppus, and engraved by B. Cole.* London, 1737. (26cm)

Park 31

Bell, Robert (1731?-84), bookseller, Philadelphia, Pa. Architecture Displayed, containing the most useful and Requisite Problems in Geometry, by Hoppus. ¶ *Catalogue* (1783), p. 14.

Hall, David (1714-72), bookseller, Philadelphia, Pa. Hoppus's Architecture. Quarto. ¶ *Catalogue* (1754), broadside. Advertised for sale again in 1761, 1763, 1767, 1768, and 1769.

Hall, William (1752-1834), bookseller, Philadelphia, Pa.
   Hoppus's Architecture. Quarto. ¶ *Catalogue* (1774?), broadsheet.

New York, N.Y., Society Library
   Hoppus's Architecture. Folio. ¶ *The charter, and bye-laws, of the New-York Society Library; with a catalogue of the books* (New York: Gaine, 1773), p. 22.
   EAI: E12895; W88

Rivington, James (1724-1802), bookseller, New York, N.Y., & Philadelphia, Pa.
   Hoppus's Builder's Repository. ¶ *Catalogue* (1760), p. 45.

Rivington, James (1724-1802), & Samuel Brown (fl. 1755-69), booksellers, New York, N.Y., & Philadelphia, Pa.
   Hoppus's Builder's Repository. ¶ *Catalogue* (1762), p. 67.

47. Hoppus, Edward (d. 1739). *Practical measuring made easy to the meanest capacity, by a new set of tables; which shew at sight, the solid or superficial content (and consequently the value) of any piece or quantity of squared or round timber, be it standing or felled, also of stone, board, glass &c. made use of in the erecting or repairing of any building, &c. Contrived to answer all the occasions of gentlemen and artificers, far beyond any thing yet extant: the contents being given in feet, inches, and twelth parts of an inch. With a preface; shewing the excellence of this new method of measuring, and demonstrating, that whoever ventures to rely upon those obsolete tables and directions published by Isaac Keay, is*

liable to be deceived (in common cases) 10s. in the pound. 2d ed. London, 1738. First edition, London, 1736. (19.5 x 8cm) Park 32

Allen, Thomas (fl. 1785-99), bookseller, New York, N.Y.
Hoppus's Practical Measuring made easy to the meanest capacity, by a new set of tables, which shew at first sight the solid and superficial content (and consequently the value) of any piece of squared or round timber, be it standing or felled. Duodecimo. ¶ *Catalogue* (1792), p. 24.

Beers, Isaac (1742?-1813), bookseller, New Haven, Conn.
Hoppus's Measurer. ¶ *A catalogue of books, sold by Isaac Beers* ([New Haven]: Green, 1791), p. 22.
EAI: E46123; W146

Campbell, Robert (d. 1800), bookseller, Philadelphia, Pa.
Hoppus's measurer, greatly enlarged and improved. ¶ *Robert Campbell's sale catalogue of books* ([Philadelphia, 1791]), p. 34. Advertised for sale again in 1797. EAI: E23244; W147

Campbell, Samuel (1763?-1836), bookseller, New York, N.Y.
Hoppus's Practical Measuring, made easy to the meanest capacities, by a new set of tables. Octavo. ¶ *Samuel Campbell's sale catalogue for 1787* (New York: Campbell, 1787), p. 19. Advertised for sale again in 1794 and 1798. EAI: E20260; W114

Carey, Mathew (1760-1839), bookseller, Philadelphia, Pa.
Hoppus's practical measuring, made easy to the

meanest capacity, by a new set of tables. Octavo. ¶ *Catalogue* (1794), p. 51.

Childs, Francis (1763-1830), & Company, booksellers, New York, N.Y.
Hoppus's Measurer, enlarged and improved. ¶ *Catalogue* (1793), p. 20.

Cox, Edward (fl. 1766-78), & Edward Berry (fl. 1766-72), booksellers, Boston, Mass.
Hoppus's Measuring. Octavo. ¶ *Catalogue* (1772?), p. 15.

Dunlap, William (d. 1779), bookseller, Philadelphia, Pa.
Hoppus's Practical Measuring. ¶ *Catalogue* (1760), n.p.

Knox, Henry (1750-1806), bookseller, Boston, Mass.
Hopus's Measuring. ¶ *Catalogue* (1773), p. 19.

Mein, John (fl. 1760-75), bookseller, Boston, Mass.
Hoppus's measuring. London, 1761. ¶ *Catalogue* (1765), p. 56. Advertised for sale in 1766.

Noel, Garrat (fl. 1752-75), bookseller, New York, N.Y., & Philadelphia, Pa.
Hoppus's Practical Measurer. ¶ *Catalogue* (1762), p. 27.

Payne, Jonas, & Philip Hearn, booksellers, Savannah, Ga.
Hoppus's practical measuring made easy. Duodecimo. ¶ *A catalogue of books to be sold* ([Savannah: Johnston, 1790]), broadside.   EAI: E22755; W141

Rice, Henry (d. 1804), & Patrick (fl. 1792-1804), booksellers, Philadelphia, Pa.
 Hoppus' measuring. Duodecimo. ¶ *Catalogue* (1795), p. 59. Advertised for sale again in 1796.

Ross, Joseph, & George Douglas, booksellers, Petersburgh, Va.
 Hoppus's Measuring made Easy to the meanest Capacity in a new set of Tables, &c. Octavo. ¶ *A catalogue of books, &c. now selling by Ross & Douglas* (Petersburgh [Va.], Jan. 1800), p. 15.
         EAI: E38237; W284

Sparhawk, John (1730-1803), bookseller, Philadelphia, Pa.
 Hoppus's measurer. Octavo. ¶ *Catalogue* (1774?), p. 14.

Spotswood, William (1753?-1805), bookseller, Boston, Mass., & Philadelphia, Pa.
 Hoppus's practical measuring made easy. ¶ *Catalogue* (1795), p. 55.

Thomas, Isaiah (1749-1831), bookseller, Worcester, Mass., Boston, Mass., & Albany, N.Y.
 Hoppus's Measurer. Duodecimo. ¶ *Catalogue of books to be sold by Isaiah Thomas, at his bookstore in Worcester, Massachusetts* (Worcester: Thomas & Worcester, 1792), p. 21. EAI: E24845; W165

Thomas, Isaiah (1749-1831), Isaiah Thomas, Jr. (1773-1819), & Alexander Thomas (1775-1809), booksellers, Worcester, Mass.
 Hoppus's Measurer. Duodecimo. ¶ *Catalogue of*

books to be sold by *Thomas, Son & Thomas* (Worcester: Thomas, Son & Thomas, 1796), p. 37.
EAI: E31290; W229

White, James (1755-1824), bookseller, Boston, Mass.
Hoppus's Measurer. ¶ *Catalogue* (1797?), p. 15.

48. Hutton, Charles (1737-1823). *The principles of bridges: containing the mathematical demonstrations of the properties of the arches, the thickness of the piers, the force of the water against them, &c. Together with practical observations and directions drawn from the whole.* Newcastle, 1772. (22cm)

    Carey, Mathew (1760-1839), bookseller, Philadelphia, Pa.
    Hutton's principles of bridges, containing mathematical demonstrations of the properties of the arches, the thickness of the piers, the force of the arches against them, &c. together with practical observations and directions drawn from the whole, stitched in blue paper. Octavo. ¶ *Catalogue* (1794), p. 61.

    New York, N.Y., Society Library
    Hutton's (Charles) principles of bridges (pamphlet). Octavo. ¶ *Continuation of the catalogue of the New-York Society Library* ([New York: Gaine, 1791]), p. 90.   EAI: E23618; W150

49. Jones, Inigo (1573-1652). *The most notable antiquity of Great Britain, vulgarly called Stoneheng on Salisbury Plain. Restored, by Inigo Jones esquire, architect generall to the king.* London, 1655. (28.5cm)

    Cambell, Duncan (fl. 1693-95), bookseller, Boston, Mass.

Jones's Antiquity of Great Britain. Folio. ¶ *Catalogue* [of the library of Samuel Lee] (1693), p. 10.

Charleston, S.C., Library Society
Jones's (Inigo) account of Stonehenge. London, 1725. Folio. ¶ *Catalogue* (1770), p. 7.

Philadelphia, Pa., Library Company
The most notable Antiquity of Great-Britain, vulgarly called Stone-Heng, on Salisbury Plain, restored, by Inigo Jones, Esq; Architect General to the King. To which are added, The Chorea Gigantum, or Stone-Heng restored to the Danes, by Dr. Charleton; and Mr. Webb's Vindication of Stone-Heng restored, in Answer to Dr. Charleton's Reflections; with Observations upon the Orders and Rules of Architecture in Use among the antient Romans. Before the Whole are prefixed certain Memoirs relating to the Life of Inigo Jones; with his Effigies, engraved by Hollar; as also Doctor Charleton's, by P. Lombart; and four new Views of Stone-Heng, in its present Situation; with above 20 other Copper- plates, and a compleat Index to the entire Collection. London, 1725. ¶ *Catalogue* (1757), p. 12.

50. Jones, William (d. 1757). *The gentlemens or builders companion containing variety of usefull designs for doors, gateways, peers, pavilions, temples, chimney-pieces, and other decorations by Wm. Jones archt. Part the first illustrated with 31 copper-plates neatly engrav'd.* [London?, ca.1735?]. (25cm)

Knox, Henry (1750-1806), bookseller, Boston, Mass.

Architectural Books in Early America

Jones designs for chimney ceilings, &c. ¶ *Catalogue* (1773), p. 21.

51. Jores, J. *A new book of iron work, containing a great variety of designs (useful for painters, cabinet-makers, carvers, smiths, fillegre-piercers, &c.) with gates of various sorts, pilasters, fence for beaufets, tables, rails, stair-cases, galleries, balconies, sign and lamp irons, door-lights, gratings, brackets, pedestals, weather-cocks, spindles, &c. The whole neatly engraved on twenty copper-plates, design'd by J. Jores.* [London, 1759]. (34cm) Park 34

Bell, Robert (1731?-84), bookseller, Philadelphia, Pa.
J[or]es's Designs for Iron Work on 20 Copper plates.
¶ *A catalogue of new and old books* ([Boston, 1770), broadside. Advertised for sale again in 1773 as Jores's *Ornamental designs*, folio.   EAI: E42060; W72

Noel, Garrat (fl. 1752-75), bookseller, New York, N.Y.
New Designs for Iron Works, useful for Smith's, Carver's, Cabinet-makers, &c. ¶ *Catalogue* (1762), p. 27.

Noel, Garrat (fl. 1752-75), & Ebenezer Hazard (1744-1817), booksellers, New York, N.Y.
Jores's new Book of Iron Work, containing a Variety of Designs for Gates, Rails, Stair-Cases, Signs, &c. ¶ *Catalogue* (1771), p. 18.

Rivington, James (1724-1802), & Samuel Brown (fl. 1755-69), booksellers, New York, N.Y., & Philadelphia, Pa.
A new Book of Iron Work, containing a great

Variety of Designs, useful for Painters, Cabinet Makers, Carvers, Smiths with Gates of various Sorts; Pilasters, Fences for Beaufets, Tables, Rails, Stair-Cases, Galleries, Balconies, Sign and Lamp Irons, Door Lights, Gratings, Brackets, Pedestals, Weather-Cocks, Spindles, &c. on Twenty Copper Plates, by J. Jones. ¶ *Catalogue* (1762), p. 66.

52. Keay, Isaac (fl. 1730?). *The practical measurer, his pocket-companion: containing tables ready cast up, for the speedy mensuration of timber, board, &c. being very useful for such as are necessarily employ'd in the practice of measuring. By Isaac Keay. The fourth edition, revised and corrected, and thereto added columns for the side of the square, being inches, and 1 and 3 quarters, or double to what they were before, &c. With an appendix, containing four several ways of measuring both timber of one thickness and tapering, and a vindication of measuring by the girt; and a preface. By E. Hutton, gent.* 4th ed. London, 1730. First edition 1718. (18 x 8cm)   Park 35

Hall, David (1714-72), bookseller, Philadelphia, Pa.
    Keay's measuring. ¶ *Catalogue* (1763?), broadsheet.

Noel, Garrat (fl. 1752-75), bookseller, New York, N.Y.
    Keay's Practical Measurer. ¶ *A catalogue of books in history, divinity, law, arts and sciences* (New York: Gaine, 1755), p. 12.   EAI: E7519; W26

Rivington, James (1724-1802), & Samuel Brown (fl. 1755-69), booksellers, New York, N.Y., & Philadelphia, Pa.
    Keay's Art of Measuring. ¶ *Catalogue* (1762), p. 46.

53. Kent, William (1684-1748). *The designs of Inigo Jones, consisting of plans and elevations for publick and private buildings. Publish'd by William Kent, with some additional designs.* 2 vols. in 1. London, 1727. (43cm)   Park 36

> Bradford, Thomas (1745-1838), bookseller, Philadelphia, Pa.
>> Jone's architecture. ¶ *Catalogue* (1796), p. 56. Identified as Kent's *The designs of Inigo Jones* by Johnston, although it may also be identified as Ware's *Designs of Inigo Jones.*

> Philadelphia, Pa., Library Company
>> The designs of Inigo Jones, consisting of plans and elevations for public and private buildings. Published by William Kent, with some additional designs. 2 vols. in one. London, 1770. Folio. ¶ *Supplement to the catalogue of books, belonging to the Library Company of Philadelphia* (Philadelphia: Poulson, 1793), p. 28.   EAI: E25995; W177

54. Laing, David (1774-1856). *Hints for dwellings: consisting of original designs for cottages, farm-houses, villas, &c. plain and ornamental; with plans to each: in which strict attention is paid to unite convenience and elegance with economy. Including some designs for town houses. By D. Laing, architect and surveyor. Elegantly engraved, in aqua-tinta, on thirty-four plates, with appropriate scenery.* London, 1800. (32cm)

> Fenno, John Ward (1778-1802), bookseller, New York, N.Y.
>> Laing's Cottages, including some designs for Town-

houses, . . . 34 plates, elegantly engraved in aqua tinta, with appropriate scenery. Quarto. ¶ *Catalogue* (1800), p. 4.

55. Langley, Batty (1696-1751). *Ancient masonry, both in the theory and practice, demonstrating the useful rules of arithmetick, geometry, and architecture, in the proportions and orders of the most eminent masters of all nations, viz. Vitruvius, Bramante, Julio Romano, Michael Angelo, Carlo Cesare Osio, Andrea Palladio, Vincent Scamozzi, M. J. Barozzio of Vignola, Sebastian Serlio, Daniel Barbaro, L. B. Alberti, P. Cataneo, P. de Lorme, Viola, J. Bullant, Julian Mau-Clerc, J. Berain, Sebastian le Clerc, Claude Perault, Inigo Jones, Sir Christoph. Wren, &c. &c. &c. And also of the Cariatides, Persians, French, Spanish, and English. Together with their most valuable designs for temples, triumphal arches, portico's, colonades, piazza's, arcades, frontispieces, gates and doors, windows, niches, entablatures, pediments, capitals, festoons, trophies, ballusters, balconies, ballustrades, cieling-pieces, chimney-pieces, floors, pavements, arches, groins, stair-cases, roofs, obelisques, ornaments, &c. The whole interspersed with critical remarks and observations on each master, illustrated by above three thousand examples, engraved on four hundred and ninety four large folio copper plates. With a dictionarial index, explaining the terms of art used herein.* 2 vols. London, 1736. (49cm)   Park 37

Earlier edition published under the title: *The principles of ancient masonry.* London, 1733.

Bell, Robert (1731?-84), bookseller, Philadelphia, Pa.
   Langley's Antient Masonry, both in the Theory and Practice, demonstrating the useful rules of Arith-

metic, Geometry, and Architecture, in the Proportions and Orders of the most eminent Masters of all Nations. With critical Remarks and Observations on each Master, illustrated by above three Thousand Examples, engraved on 494 large folio Copperplates. 2 vols. Folio. ¶ *Catalogue* (1773), p. [48].

Philadelphia, Pa., Library Company
Masonry, (Ancient) both in theory and practice; demonstrating the useful rules of arithmetick, geometry and architecture, in the proportions and orders of the most eminent Masters of all nations, together with their most valuable designs; illustrated by above 3000 examples, engraved on 494 large copper plates: with a dictionarial Index, explaining the terms of art used therein. By B. Langley. 2 vols. London, 1736. Folio. ¶ *Catalogue* (1770), n.p.

Philadelphia, Pa., Union Library Company
Ancient Masonry, in Theory and Practice, illustrated by above Three Thousand Examples, engraved on 494 large Copper Plates, by B. Langley. 1736. Folio. ¶ *Catalogue* (1765), p. 1.

56. Langley, Batty (1696-1751). *The builder's chest-book; or a complete key to the five orders of columns in architecture. Where by way of dialogue in nine lectures the etymology, characters, proportions, profiles, ornaments, measures and dispositions of the members of their several columns and entablatures are distinctly consider'd and explain'd with respect to the practice of Palladio. Together with the manner of drawing the geometrical elevation of the five orders of columns in architecture, and to measure the several parts of*

buildings in general. The whole exemplified by way of dialogue, in a very concise and familiar manner, illustrated on seven copperplates: being a necessary companion for gentlemen, as well as masons, carpenters, joyners, bricklayers, plasterers, painters, &c. and all others concern'd in the several parts of buildings in general. London, 1727. (17cm)

Park 38

Knox, Henry (1750-1806), bookseller, Boston, Mass.
    Langley's Chest Book or Key to the 5 Orders. ¶ *Catalogue* (1773), p. 23.

Rivington, James (1724-1802), bookseller, New York, N.Y., & Philadelphia, Pa.
    Langley's Builder's Chest Book. ¶ *Catalogue* (1760), p. 45.

Rivington, James (1724-1802), & Samuel Brown (fl. 1755-69), booksellers, New York, N.Y., & Philadelphia, Pa.
    Langley's Builder's Chest Book. ¶ *Catalogue* (1762), p. 67.

Russell, Joseph (1734-95), & Samuel Clap (1745-1809), auctioneers, Boston, Mass.
    Builder's Chest Book. Octavo. ¶ *On Tuesday morning, 16th October... will be sold... the following collection of books* ([Boston, 1792]), broadside.

EAI: E46568; W164

57. Langley, Batty (1696-1751). *The builder's compleat assistant, or, a library of arts and sciences, absolutely necessary to be understood by builders and workmen in general. Viz. I.*

Arithmetick, vulgar and decimal in whole numbers and fractions. II. Geometry, lineal, superficial and solid. III. Architecture, universal. IV. Mensuration. V. Plain trigonometry. VI. Surveying of land, &c. VII. Mechanick powers. VIII. Hydrostaticks. Illustrated by above thirteen hundred examples of lines, superficies, solids, mouldings, pedestals, columns, pilasters, entablatures, pediments, imposts, block cornices, rustick quoins, frontispieces, arcades, portico's, &c. proportioned by modules and minutes, according to Andrea Palladio, and by equal parts. Likewise, great varieties of trussed roofs, timber bridges, centerings, arches, groins, twisted rails, compartments, obelisques, vases, pedestals for busto's, sun-dials, fonts, &c. and methods for raising heavy bodies by the force of levers, pulleys, axis in peritrochio, screws, and wedges; as also water, by the common pump, crane, &c. wherein the properties, and pressure of the air, on water, &c. is explained. The whole exemplified by 77 large copper-plates. 2d ed. 2 vols. London, [ca. 1740]. First edition, London, 1738. (24cm) Park 39

Bell, Robert (1731?-84), bookseller, Philadelphia, Pa.
Langley's Builders Complete Assistant, being a Library of Arts and Sciences, absolutely necessary to be understood by Builders and Workmen in general, exemplified by 77 large Quarto Copperplates. 2 vols. Quarto. ¶ *Catalogue* (1773), p. 11. Advertised for sale again in 1783.

Cox, Edward (fl. 1766-78), & Edward Berry (fl. 1766-72), booksellers, Boston, Mass.
Langley's Assistant. 2 vols. Octavo. ¶ *Catalogue* (1772?), p. 16.

Fenno, John Ward (1778-1802), bookseller, New York, N.Y.
    Langley's Builder's Assistant, . . . 77 large 4to plates. 2 vols. Octavo. ¶ *Catalogue* (1800), p. 6.

Guild, Benjamin (1749-92), bookseller, Boston, Mass.
    Langley's complete assistant. 2 vols. Duodecimo [?]. ¶ *Catalogue* (1787?; E45266), p. 11. Advertised for sale again in 1789.

Hall, David (1714-72), bookseller, Philadelphia, Pa.
    Langley's Builders Compleat Assistant. Quarto. ¶ *Lately imported, and to be sold by David Hall* ([Philadelphia: Franklin & Hall, 1761?]), broadside. EAI: E9997; W42

Larkin, Ebenezer (1767-1813), bookseller, Boston, Mass.
    Langley's Builder's Assistant. 2 vols. ¶ *Catalogue* (1793), p. 46. Advertised for sale again in 1798.

Noel, Garrat (fl. 1752-75), & Ebenezer Hazard (1744-1817), booksellers, New York, N.Y.
    Langley's Builder's Assistant. ¶ *Catalogue* (1771), p. 18.

Providence, R.I., Providence Library
    Langley's Builder's Assistant. 2 vols. Octavo. ¶ *Catalogue* (1768), p. 11.

Thomas, Isaiah (1749-1831), & Ebenezer Turrell Andrews (1766-1851), booksellers, Boston, Mass.
    Langley's Builder's Assistant. 2 vols. Octavo. ¶ *Catalogue* (1793), p. 46.

West, David (1765-1810), bookseller, Boston, Mass.
  Langley's Builder's Assistant. 2 vols. Octavo. ¶ *Catalogue* (1793), p. 46.

58. Langley, Batty (1696-1751). *The builder's director, or benchmate: being a pocket-treasury of the Grecian, Roman, and Gothic orders of architecture, made easy to the meanest capacity by near five hundred examples. Improved from the best authors, ancient and modern, of pedestals, bases, shafts, capitals, columns, architraves, freezes, brackets, cornices, arches, imposts, key-stones, trusses, moldings of raking pediments, frontispieces, portico's, arcades, colonades, chimney-pieces, fretts, guilochi's, groins, weatherings, moldings for tabernacles, frames, &c. proportioned by minutes and by equal parts, the like never before published. Engraved on 184 copper plates, wherein the orders of Andrea Palladio are truly laid down, free from erroneous measures. Written for the use of gentlemen delighting in true architecture; and for masters and workmen to draw from and work after.* London, 1747. (16cm) Park 40

Bell, Robert (1731?-83), bookseller, Philadelphia, Pa.
  Langley's Builder's Director. ¶ *Catalogue* (1783), p. 52.

Cox, Edward (fl. 1766-78), & Edward Berry (fl. 1766-72), booksellers, Boston, Mass.
  Langley's Builder's Director or Benchmate. Duodecimo. ¶ *Catalogue* (1772?), p. 17.

Fenno, John Ward (1778-1802), bookseller, New York, N.Y.
  Langley's Bench Mate, . . . 184 plates. Duodecimo. ¶

Catalogue (1800), p. 6.

Knox, Henry (1750-1806), bookseller, Boston, Mass.
Langley's Director, or Benchmate. ¶ *Catalogue* (1773), p. 23.

Mein, John (fl. 1760-75), bookseller, Boston, Mass.
Langley's Builders Director. ¶ *A catalogue of curious and valuable books* ([Boston: McAlpine?, 1766]), p. 32.
EAI: E41642; W59

Noel, Garrat (fl. 1752-75), bookseller, New York, N.Y.
The Builder's Director, or Benchmate. ¶ *Catalogue* (1762), p. 27.

Noel, Garrat (fl. 1752-75), & Ebenezer Hazard (1744-1817), booksellers, New York, N.Y.
Langley's Builder's Director, or Bench Mate. ¶ *Catalogue* (1771), p. 18.

Thomas, Isaiah (1749-1831), Ebenezer Turrell Andrews (1766-1851), & Obadiah Penniman (1776-1820), booksellers, Albany, N.Y.
Langley's Builder's Directory and Bench Mate. ¶ *Catalogue* (1797?), p. 34.

59. Langley, Batty (1696-1751), & Thomas Langley (1702-51). *The builder's jewel: or, the youth's instructor, and workman's remembrancer. Explaining short and easy rules, made familiar to the meanest capacity, for drawing and working, I. The five orders of columns entire; or any part of an order, without regard to the module or diameter. And to enrich them with their rusticks, flutings, cablings, dentules, modi-*

lions, &c. Also to proportion their doors, windows, intercolumnations, portico's, and arcades. Together with fourteen varieties of raking, circular, scroll'd, compound, and contracted pediments; and the true formation and accadering of their raking and returned cornices; and mouldings for tabernacle frames, pannelling, and centering for groins, truss'd partitions, girders, roofs, and domes. With a section of the dome of St. Paul's, London. The whole illustrated by upwards of 200 examples, engraved on 100 copper-plates. London, 1741. (13.5cm)   Park 41

Allen, Thomas (fl. 1785-99), bookseller, New York, N.Y.
    Langley's Builder's Jewel, or the Youth's Instructor and Workman's Remembrancer, &c. ¶ *Catalogue* (1792), p. 26.

Beers, Isaac (1742?-1813), bookseller, New Haven, Conn.
    Langley's Builder's Jewel. ¶ *Catalogue* (1791), p. 22.

Bell, Robert (1731?-84), bookseller, Philadelphia, Pa.
    Langley's Builders Jewel, containing 200 Examples on 100 Copperplates. Octavo. ¶ *Catalogue* (1773), p. 16. Advertised for sale again in 1783.

Blake, William Pynson (1769-1820), bookseller, Boston, Mass.
    Langley's Builder's Jewel. ¶ *Catalogue* (1793), p. 25. Advertised for sale again in 1796.

Blake, William Pynson (1769-1820), & Lemuel (1775-1861), booksellers, Boston, Mass.
    Langley's Builder's Jewel. ¶ *Catalogue* (1798), p. 26.

Carey, Mathew (1760-1839), bookseller, Philadelphia, Pa.
Langley's builder's jewel, or the youth's instructor and workman's remembrancer, illustrated with 100 copperplates. Duodecimo. ¶ *Catalogue* (1794), p. 61.

Cox, Edward (fl. 1766-78), & Edward Berry (fl. 1766-72), booksellers, Boston, Mass.
Langley's Builder's Jewell. Duodecimo. ¶ *Catalogue* (1772?), p. 16.

Dabney, John (1752-1819), bookseller, Salem, Mass.
Langley's Builder's Jewel. ¶ *Additional catalogue of books, for sale or circulation, at the Salem Bookstore* (Salem, 1794), p. 18. EAI: E26840; W186

Gaine, Hugh (1726-1807), bookseller, New York, N.Y.
Builder's Jewel. ¶ *Just imported in the last vessels from London, and to be sold, by Hugh Gaine* ([New York: Gaine, 1771]), broadside. EAI: E42237; W75

Guild, Benjamin (1749-92), bookseller, Boston, Mass.
Langley's Builder's Jewel. Duodecimo. ¶ *Catalogue* (1787?; E45266), p. 11. Advertised for sale again in 1789.

Hall, David (1714-74), bookseller, Philadelphia, Pa.
Langley's builder's jewel. Duodecimo. ¶ *Catalogue* (1760?), broadside. Advertised for sale again in 1761, 1763, 1768, and 1769.

Hall, William (1752-1834), bookseller, Philadelphia, Pa.
Langley's Builders Jewel. Duodecimo. ¶ *Catalogue* (1774?), broadsheet.

Knox, Henry (1750-1806), bookseller, Boston, Mass.
Langley's Builder's Jewell. Duodecimo. ¶ *Catalogue* (1773), p. 23.

Larkin, Ebenezer (1767-1813), bookseller, Boston, Mass.
Langley's Builder's Jewel. Duodecimo. ¶ *Catalogue* (1793), p. 46.

Mein, John (fl. 1760-75), bookseller, Boston, Mass.
Langley's Builder's Jewel. London, 1763. ¶ *Catalogue* (1765), p. 32. Advertised for sale again in 1766.

Nancrede, Paul Joseph Guérard de (1760-1841), bookseller, Boston, Mass.
Builder's jewel. Quarto. ¶ *Joseph Nancrede's catalogue of books* ([Boston, 1796]), p. 5. Advertised for sale again in 1798.   EAI: E30833; W220

New York, N.Y., Society Library
Builder's jewel. Duodecimo. ¶ *Catalogue* (1792), p. 111.

Prichard, William (fl.1782-1809), bookseller, Philadelphia, Pa.
Langley's Builder's Jewel, illustrated on 100 Copperplates. Duodecimo. ¶ *Catalogue* (1785), p. 23.

Rice, Henry (d. 1804), & Company, booksellers, Philadelphia, Pa.
Langley's Builder's Jewel. ¶ *Catalogue* (1790?), p. 43.

Rice, Henry (d. 1804), & Patrick (fl. 1792-1804), booksellers, Philadelphia, Pa.

Langley's builders jewel, with cuts. Duodecimo. ¶ *Catalogue* (1795), p. 59. Advertised for sale again in 1796.

Rivington, James (1724-1802), bookseller, New York, N.Y., & Philadelphia, Pa.
Langley's Builder's Jewell. ¶ *Catalogue* (1760), p. 45.

Rivington, James (1724-1802), & Samuel Brown (fl. 1755-69), booksellers, New York, N.Y., & Philadelphia, Pa.
Langley's Builder's Jewel. ¶ *Catalogue* (1762), p. 67.

Thomas, Isaiah (1749-1831), & Ebenezer Turrell Andrews (1766-1851), booksellers, Boston, Mass.
Langley's Builder's Jewel. Duodecimo. ¶ *Catalogue* (1793), p. 46.

Thomas, Isaiah (1749-1831), Ebenezer Turrell Andrews (1766-1851), & Obadiah Penniman (1776-1820), booksellers, Albany, N.Y.
Langley's Builders' Jewel, or Youth's Instructor. ¶ *Catalogue* (1797?), p. 34.

West, David (1765-1810), bookseller, Boston, Mass.
Langley's Builder's Jewel. Duodecimo. ¶ *Catalogue* (1793), p. 46.

60. Langley, Batty (1696-1751). *The city and country builder's, and workman's treasury of designs: or, the art of drawing, and working the ornamental parts of architecture. Illustrated, by upwards of four hundred grand designs, for peirs, gates, doors, windows, niches, buffets, cisterns, chimney pieces,*

tabernacle frames, pavements, frets, gulochi's, pulpits, types, altar pieces, monuments, fonts, obelisques, pedestals, for sundials, busto's, and stone tables, book cases, ciellings, and iron works. Finely engraved on 186 large quarto plates; proportioned by aliquot parts: to which are prefix'd, the five orders of columns; according to Andrea Palladio, whose members are proportioned by aliquot parts, in a more easy manner, than has been yet done. The whole interspersed, with sure rules, for working, all the varieties of raking members in pediments, modilions, &c. The like, for the immediate use of workmen never published before, in any language. London, 1740. (28.5cm) Park 42

Bell, Robert (1731?-84), bookseller, Philadelphia, Pa.
Langley's City and Country Builder's and Workman's Treasury of Designs: Or, the art of drawing or working the ornamental Parts of Architecture, illustrated by upwards of 400 grand Designs, neatly engraved on 186 Copperplates; also an Appendix of 14 large Copperplates of Trusses for Girders and Beams, different Sorts of Rafters, and a Variety of Roofs. Folio. ¶ *Catalogue* (1773), p. 3.

Blake, William Pynson (1769-1820), bookseller, Boston, Mass.
Langley's Designs in Architecture. ¶ *Catalogue* (1793), p. 25.

Bradford, William (1719-91), auctioneer, Philadelphia, Pa.
Langley's City and Country Builders and Workmans Treasury of Designs. ¶ *Catalogue* (1760?), p. 9.

Hall, David (1714-72), bookseller, Philadelphia, Pa.

Langley's Builder's and Tradesman's Treasury of Designs. Quarto. ¶ *Catalogue* (1754), broadside. Advertised for sale again in 1760 and 1761.

Knox, Henry (1750-1806), bookseller, Boston, Mass.
Langley's Treasury of designs. Quarto. ¶ *Catalogue* (1773), p. 23.

Philadelphia, Pa., Loganian Library
The city and country builder's and workman's treasury of designs; or, the art of drawing and working the ornamental parts of architecture; with plates. London, 1745. Quarto. ¶ *Catalogue of the books belonging to the Loganian Library* (Philadelphia: Poulson, 1795), p. 33.   EAI: E29314; W203

Rivington, James (1724-1802), bookseller, New York, N.Y., & Philadelphia, Pa.
Langley's Builder's Treasury, Designs for Builders and other Artists. ¶ *Catalogue* (1760), p. 45.

Rivington, James (1724-1802), & Samuel Brown (fl. 1755-69), booksellers, New York, N.Y., & Philadelphia, Pa.
Langley's Builder's Treasury, designs for Builders and other Artists. ¶ *Catalogue* (1762), p. 66.

61. Langley, Batty (1696-1751), & Thomas Langley (1702-51). *Gothick architecture, improved by rules and proportions. In many grand designs of columns, doors, windows, chimneypieces, arcades, colonades, porticos, umbrellos, temples, and pavillions &c. with plans, elevations and profiles; geometrically explained.* London, 1747. (30.5cm)

Earlier edition published under the title: *Ancient architecture, restored, and improved, by a great variety of grand and useful designs entirely new in the Gothic mode for the ornamenting of buildings and gardens exceeding everything thats extant. Exquisitely engraved on LXIV large quarto copper plates and printed on superfine royal paper.* [London, 1742]. (30.5cm)

Noel, Garrat (fl. 1752-75), & Ebenezer Hazard (1744-1817), booksellers, New York, N.Y.
Langley's Gothic Architecture.   ¶ *Catalogue* (1771), p. 18.

62. Langley, Batty (1696-1751). *The London prices of bricklayers materials and works, both of new buildings and repairs, justly ascertained: and the common exactions and abuses therein detected. Interspersed with rules for estimating, performing and measuring all kinds of plain, circular, elliptical, Gothick, spherical, spheroidal, conical and pyramidical brick-works: wherein the abutments of all sorts of arches, and the manner of building brick-flooring for the prevention of fire, is clearly explained. The whole arithmetically and geometrically demonstrated. Also illustrated with a great variety of designs for plain and rusticated piers, for gates, piazzas, &c. In thirty-two curious copper plates. Written for the use of gentlemen, stewards, and workmen in general, and particularly for such landlords and tenants who are subject to the repairs of buildings.* London, 1748. (21cm)
Park 109

Cox, Edward (fl. 1766-78), & Edward Berry (fl. 1766-72),

booksellers, Boston, Mass.
> Langley's London Prices of Bricklayers Work. Octavo. ¶ *Catalogue* (1772?), p. 17.

Stephens, Thomas (fl. 1793-97), bookseller, Philadelphia, Pa.
> Langley's London Prices of Building Materials and Work, &c. Octavo. ¶ *Stephens's catalogue of books, &c. for 1795* (Philadelphia: Woodward, [1795]), p. 45.
> EAI: E47610; W209

63. Langley, Batty (1696-1751). *Practical geometry applied to the useful arts of building, surveying, gardening and mensuration; calculated for the service of gentlemen as well as artisans, and set to view in four parts. Containing, I. Preliminaries or the foundations of the several arts abovementioned. II. The various orders of architecture, laid down and improved from the best masters; with the ways of making draughts of buildings, gardens, groves, fountains, &c. the laying down of maps, cities, lordships, farms, &c. III. The doctrine and rules of mensuration of all kinds, illustrated by select examples in buildings, gardening, timber, &c. IV. Exact tables of mensuration, shewing, by inspection, the superficial and solid contents of all kinds of bodies, without the fatigue of arithmetical computation: to which is annexed, an account of the clandestine practice now generally obtaining in mensuration, and particularly the damage sustained in selling timber by measure. The whole exemplifi'd with above 60 folio copper plates, by the best hands.* London, 1726. (34.5cm)   Park 44

Philadelphia, Pa., Library Company
> Practical Geometry, apply'd to the useful Arts of

Architectural Books in Early America

Building, Gardening, Mensuration, &c. calculated for the Use of Gentlemen as well as Artisans. By Batty Langley. 2d ed. London, 1729. Folio. ¶ *Books added to the library since the year 1741* ([Philadelphia: Franklin, 1746]), p. 3.   EAI: E5853; W19

64. Langley, Batty (1696-1751). *The workman's golden rule for drawing and working the five orders in architecture. Wherein their pedestals, columns, entablatures, imposts, and arches, are taken from the best examples of the ancients, and proportioned by equal parts, in a more concise, accurate, and easy manner, than has been done in any language. For the instruction of apprentices and journeymen, masons, bricklayers, carpenters, joiners, carvers, turners, painters, plaisterers, cabinet-makers, &c. (and such masters) who are unacquainted with so much architecture, as is absolutely necessary for them to understand, in their respective professions: and others, who desire a just knowledge of the fundamental rules of that noble art.* London, 1750. (10cm)
Park 45

Bell, Robert (1731?-84), bookseller, Philadelphia, Pa.
   Langley's Workman's Golden Rule for the 5 Orders. ¶ *Catalogue* (1783), p. 52.

Cox, Edward (fl. 1766-78), & Edward Berry (fl. 1766-72), booksellers, Boston, Mass.
   Langley's Workman's Golden Rule. Duodecimo. ¶ *Catalogue* (1772?), p. 17.

Hall, David (1714-74), bookseller, Philadelphia, Pa.
   Golden Rule. ¶ *Catalogue* (1763?), broadsheet. Advertised for sale again in 1767, 1768, and 1769 as

Langley's workman's golden rule.

Rivington, James (1724-1802), bookseller, New York, N.Y., & Philadelphia, Pa.
    Langley's Builder's Golden Rule. ¶ *Catalogue* (1760), p. 45.

Rivington, James (1724-1802), & Samuel Brown (fl. 1755-69), booksellers, New York, N.Y., & Philadelphia, Pa.
    Langley's Builder's Golden Rule. ¶ *Catalogue* (1762), p. 67.

65. Laugier, Marc Antoine, abbé (1713-69). *Essai sur l'architecture.* Paris, 1753. (17cm)

An essay on architecture; in which its true principles are explained, and invariable rules proposed for directing the judgment and forming the taste of the gentleman and the architect, with regard to the different kinds of buildings, and embellishment of cities, and the planning of gardens. Adorned with a frontispiece, designed by Mr. Wale, and curiously engraven. London, 1755. (17.5cm)

Bell, Robert (1731?-84), bookseller, Philadelphia, Pa.
    Essai sur L'Architecture par Laugier. ¶ *Catalogue* (1783), p. 11.

66. Le Clerc, Sébastien (1637-1714). *Traité d'architecture avec des remarques et des observations tres-utiles pour les jeunes gens, qui veulent s'appliquer à ce bel art.* 2 vols. in 1. Paris, 1714. (25cm)   Park 46

A treatise of architecture, with remarks and observations. Necessary for young people, who wou'd apply themselves to that noble art. Volume 2 includes the subtitle: *Engraven in two hundred copper plates by John Sturt. Translated by Mr. Chambers.* 2 vols. in 1. London, 1723-24. (20cm)
Park 46

Bell, Robert (1731?-84), bookseller, Philadelphia, Pa.
Le Clerc's Observations on Architecture. ¶ *Catalogue* (1783), p. 50.

Noel, Garrat (fl. 1752-75), bookseller, New York, N.Y.
Le Clerc's Architecture. ¶ *Catalogue* (1759), p. 7.

Salem, Mass., Social Library
Le Clerc's Architecture. 2 vols. Octavo. ¶ *Bylaws and regulations of the incorporated proprietors of the Social Library in Salem* ([Salem: Cushing, 1797?]), p. 19.   EAI: E32800; W243

67. Leoni, Giacomo (ca. 1686-1746). *The architecture of A. Palladio; in four books. Containing, a short treatise of the five orders, and the most necessary observations concerning all sorts of building, as also the different construction of private and publick houses, high-ways, bridges, market-places, xystes, and temples, with their plans, sections, and uprights. To which are added several notes and observations made by Inigo Jones, never printed before. Revis'd, design'd, and publish'd by Giocomo Leoni, a Venetian; . . . Translated from the Italian original.* 4 vols. in 5. London, 1715-19. (45.5cm)   Park 47

The 1742 edition includes: *Notes and remarks of Inigo Jones upon the fourth book of Palladio's architecture. Referred to the plates. Taken from the manuscript of the said Inigo Jones, in the library of Worcester-College, Oxford, June 23, 1741.*

Baltimore, Md., Library Company
> Leoni's Palladio. Folio. ¶ *A catalogue of the books, &c. belonging to the Library Company of Baltimore* (Baltimore: Hayes, 1797), p. 7.   EAI: E31769; W239

Blake, William Pynson (1769-1820), bookseller, Boston, Mass.
> Palladio's Architecture. ¶ *Catalogue* (1793), p. 31. This book could also be identified as Ware's *The four books of Andrea Palladio's architecture.*

Bradford, Thomas (1745-1838), bookseller, Philadelphia, Pa.
> Paladio's architecture with Jones' notes. 2 vols. Folio. ¶ *Catalogue* (1796), p. 56.

Charleston, S.C., Library Society
> Leoni's Palladio's architecture. London, 1742. Folio. ¶ *Catalogue* (1770), p. 7.

Harvard College Library, Cambridge, Mass.
> Palladio (Andr.), trd from the Italian, with notes by Inigo Jones. 3d ed. 2 vols. London, 1742. Folio. ¶ *Catalogue* (1790), p. 8.

Philadelphia, Pa., Library Company
> Palladio's Architecture, in 4 Books; Containing a short Treatise of the Five Orders, and the most necessary Observations concerning all Sorts of

Building. As also the different Constructions of private Houses, High-ways, Bridges, Market-places, Xystes, and Temples, with their Plans, Sections, and Uprights, Exemplified in a great Number of Copper Cuts. 2 vols. Folio. ¶ *Catalogue* (1741), n.p.

Yale College Library, New Haven, Conn.
Palladio's Architecture. ¶ *A catalogue of the library of Yale-College in New-Haven* (N[ew] London: Green, 1743), p. 43. Identified as Leoni's *The architecture of A. Palladio* by Park.

68. Leoni, Giacomo (ca. 1686-1746). *The architecture of Leon Battista Alberti in ten books. Of painting in three books and of statuary in one book. Translated into Italian by Cosimo Bartoli. And now first into English, and divided into three volumes by James Leoni, Venetian, architect; to which are added several designs of his own, for buildings both publick and private. Della architettura di Leon Battista Alberti libri X. Della pittura libri III. E della statua libro I. Tradotti in lingua Italiana da Cosimo Bartoli. Nova edizione divisa in tre tomi, da Giacomo Leoni Veneziano, architetto con aggiunta di varj suoi disegni di edificj publici e privati.* 3 vols. London, 1726. Volume 3 includes: *Some designs for buildings both publick and private by James Leoni, architect.* (45cm)   Park 48

Philadelphia, Pa., Library Company
Leoni's (James) Designs for Buildings, both publick and private. London, 1726. Folio. ¶ *Catalogue* (1770), n.p.

Philadelphia, Pa., Union Library Company

Architecture, by James Leone. Containing some Designs for Buildings, both Public and Private. 1726. Folio. ¶ *Catalogue* (1765), p. 1.

69. Leybourn, William (1626-1700?). *The mirror of architecture; or, the ground rules of the art of building according to Vincenzo Scamozzi, with the description and use of a joynt rule by John Brown, whereunto is added a compendium of the art of building.* London, 1669. (19.5cm) Park 49

   Burlington, N.J., Library Company
   The Mirror of Architecture; or, the ground Rules of the Art of Building, exactly laid down. By Vincent Scamozzie, Master Builder of Venice. &c. . . . By William Leyburn. 5th ed. London, 1708. (Given to the library by Daniel Smith) ¶ *The charter, laws, and catalogue of books, of the Library Company of Burlington* (Philadelphia: Dunlap, 1758), p. 11.
   EAI: E8096; W30

   Young, William (1755-1829), bookseller, Philadelphia, Pa.
   Lyburn's Art of Building. Quarto. ¶ *William Young's catalogue for 1787* ([Philadelphia: Young & M'Culloch, 1786]), p. 17.   EAI: E20173; W112

70. Lightoler, Thomas. *The gentleman and farmer's architect. A new work. Containing a great variety of useful and genteel designs. Being correct plans and elevations of parsonage and farm houses, lodges for parks, pinery, peach, hot and green houses, with the fire-wall, tan-pit, &c. particularly described. Dutch, and other barns, cow-houses, stables, sheepcots, huts, facades; with all other offices appertaining to a well-regulated farm; their situations rendered convenient, and aspects*

agreeable. With scales and tables of reference, describing the several parts, with their just dimensions and use. Designed and drawn by T. Lightoler, architect. And well engraved on twenty-five folio copper-plates. London, 1762. (28cm)

Park 50

Bell, Robert (1731?-84), bookseller, Philadelphia, Pa.
Lightoler's Gentleman's and Farmer's Architect, useful and genteel Designs, of Plans and Elevations, on 25 Copperplates. ¶ *Catalogue* (1783), p. 52.

Boston, Mass., broadside, September 30, 1766
Lightoler's Architecture. ¶ *Catalogue* (1766), broadside.

Bradford, Thomas (1745-1838), bookseller, Philadelphia, Pa.
Lightholde's gentleman farmer's architecture. ¶ *Catalogue* (1796), p. 56.

Noel, Garrat (fl. 1752-75), & Ebenezer Hazard (1744-1817), booksellers, New York, N.Y.
Gentleman and Farmer's Architecture. ¶ *Catalogue* (1771), p. 18.

71. Lock, Matthias (fl. 1740-69), & H. Copland. *A new book of ornaments with twelve leaves. Consisting of chimneys, sconces, tables, spandle pannels, spring clock cases, & stands. A chandelier & gerandole &c.* London, 1752. (29cm)

Park 8

Bradford, Thomas (1745-1838), bookseller, Philadelphia, Pa.

Architectural Books in Early America

Lock and Copland's ornaments. ¶ *Catalogue* (1796), p. 56.

Noel, Garrat (fl. 1752-75), & Ebenezer Hazard (1744-1817), booksellers, New York, N.Y.
Copeland's new Book of Ornaments. ¶ *Catalogue* (1771), p. 18.

72. Mandey, Venterus (1645-1701). *Mellificum mensionis: or, the marrow of measuring. Wherein a new and ready way is shewn how to measure glazing, painting, plastering, masonry, joyners, carpenters and brick-layers works. As also the measuring of land, and all other snperficies [sic] and solids, by vulgar arithmetick, without reducing the integers into the least denomination; giving the content of any superficie or solid, consisting of feet, inches, and parts of inches, in a fourth part of the time and labour requi[r]ed by the us[u]al way in vulgar arithmetick. Together with some choice principles and problems of geometry conducing thereto.* 2d ed. London, 1685. First edition 1682. (18.5cm)   Park 111

Cox, Thomas (fl. 1733-44), London bookseller, Boston, Mass.
Mandey of Measuring. Octavo. ¶ *A catalogue of books, in all arts and sciences, to be sold at the shop of T. Cox* (Boston, [1734]), p. 4.   EAI: E3765; W12

Rhode Island College Library [Brown University], Providence, R.I.
Mandey's Measuring. Octavo. ¶ *Catalogue* (1793), p. 20.

73. Manwaring, Robert. *The carpenter's compleat guide to the*

whole system of Gothic railing. Consisting of twenty-six entire new designs for paling, and gates of different kinds . . . adapted both for town and country, with full and plain directions to workmen for executing each design, and also the exact estimate and expense of the same. Together with an excellent receipt for making glue to fix the joints of the work, and which will resist all kinds of weather as long as any soundness remains in the wood. [London], 1765. (24cm)

White, James (1755?-1824), bookseller, Boston, Mass.
    Manwaring's Carpenters Guide. ¶ *Catalogue* (1797?), p. 20.

74. [Middleton, Charles (1756-1818?)]. *Decorations for parks and gardens. Designs for gates, garden seats, alcoves, temples, baths, entrance gates, lodges, facades, prospect towers, cattle sheds, ruins, bridges, greenhouses, &c., &c., also a hot house & hot wall: with plans & scales on 55 plates.* London, [1800?]. Both Howard Colvin and John Archer assign this work to Thomas Elison. (24cm)

Fenno, John Ward (1778-1802), bookseller, New York, N.Y.
    Decorations for Parks and Gardens, . . . 55 plates. Octavo. ¶ *Catalogue* (1800), p. 6.

75. Middleton, Charles (1756-1818). *Picturesque and architectural views for cottages, farm houses, and country villas. Engraved and designed by Charles Middleton, architect.* London, 1793. (46.5cm)

Baltimore, Md., Library Company
    Middleton's Picturesque and Architectural Views,

Architectural Books in Early America

(Plates). Folio. ¶ *Catalogue* (1797), p. 7.

Campbell, Samuel (1763?-1836), bookseller, New York, N.Y.
>Middleton's Picturesque and Architectural Views for Cottages, Farm-houses, and Country Villas—elegantly engraved. Folio. ¶ *Samuel Campbell's sale catalogue of books, for 1798 & 1799* ([New York: Campbell, 1798]), p. 23.   EAI: E35267; W249

76. Miller, John. *Andrea Palladio's Elements of architecture, restored to its original perfection, as published by him at Venice, anno 1581. With a geometrical explanation of his true principles of perspective . . . Also an entire new and approved method of finding the points of sight and distance . . . the whole illustrated by a variety of examples . . . on twenty-eight copperplates, with letter-press annexed. By J. Miller, esq.* London, 1759. First edition ca. 1748. (29cm)
>>Park 51

Blake, William Pynson (1769-1820), bookseller, Boston, Mass.
>Palladio's Elements of Architecture. ¶ *Catalogue* (1793), p. 31.

Noel, Garrat (fl. 1752-75), & Ebenezer Hazard (1744-1817), booksellers, New York, N.Y.
>Miller's Elements of Architecture. ¶ *Catalogue* (1771), p. 18.

77. Miller, John. *The country gentleman's architect, in a great variety of new designs; for cottages, farm-houses, country-houses, villas, lodges for park or garden entrances, and orna-*

mental wooden gates; with plans of the offices belonging to each design, distributed with a strict attention to convenience, elegance, and economy. Engraved on thirty-two plates; from designs drawn by J. Miller, architect. London, 1787. (26.5cm)

Fenno, John Ward (1778-1802), bookseller, New York, N.Y.
　　Miller's Country Gentleman's Architect, in a great variety of new designs for Cottages, Farm-Houses, Country-Houses, Villas, &c. &c. engraved on 32 plates. Quarto. ¶ *Catalogue* (1800), p. [3].

78. Morris, Robert (ca. 1702-54). *Architecture improved, in a collection of modern, elegant and useful designs; from slight and graceful recesses, lodges and other decorations in parks, gardens, woods or forests, to the portico, bath, observatory, and interior ornaments of superb buildings. With great variety of rich embellishments for chimneys in the taste of Inigo Jones, Mr. Kent, &c. All curiously engraved on fifty copper-plates, octavo.* London, 1755. (23cm)　　Park 52

Earlier edition published under the title: *The architectural remembrancer: being a collection of new and useful designs, of ornamental buildings and decorations. For parks, gardens, woods, &c. To which are added, a variety of chimney-pieces, after the manner of Inigo Jones, and Mr. Kent. The whole neatly engraven on fifty copper-plates, in octavo.* London, 1751. (23cm)

Bell, Robert (1731?-84), bookseller, Philadelphia, Pa.
　　Architecture on 50 Copperplates by Morris. ¶ *Catalogue* (1783), p. 11.

Architectural Books in Early America

Noel, Garrat (fl. 1752-75), bookseller, New York, N.Y.
 Morris's Architecture improved. ¶ *Catalogue* (1762), p. 27.

Noel, Garrat (fl. 1752-75), & Ebenezer Hazard (1744-1817), booksellers, New York, N.Y.
 Morris's Architecture improved. ¶ *Catalogue* (1771), p. 18.

Rivington, James (1724-1802), bookseller, New York, N.Y., & Philadelphia, Pa.
 Morris's Architecture improv'd, being a Collection of Modern and useful Designs. ¶ *Catalogue* (1760), p. 46.

Rivington, James (1724-1802), & Samuel Brown (fl. 1755-69), booksellers, New York, N.Y., & Philadelphia, Pa.
 Morris's Architecture improv'd, being a Collection of Modern and useful Designs. ¶ *Catalogue* (1762), p. 67.

79. Morris, Robert (ca. 1702-54). *Lectures on architecture. Consisting of rules founded upon harmonick and arithmetical proportions in building. Design'd as an agreeable entertainment for gentlemen: and more particularly useful to all who make architecture, or the polite arts, their study. Read to a society establish'd for the improvement of arts and sciences, and explain'd by examples on copper plates; with the proportions apply'd to practice.* 2 vols in 1. London, 1734-36. (20cm)   Park 53

Caritat, Louis Alexis Hocquet de (b. 1752), bookseller,

New York, N.Y.
> Morris' Robert, Lectures on Architecture, consisting of rules founded on harmonic and Arithmetical proportions in building, designed as an agreeable entertainment for gentlemen. ¶ *The feast of reason and the flow of soul. A new explanatory catalogue of H. Caritat's general & increasing circulating library* (New York: Davis, 1799), p. 72. EAI: E35279; W261

Knox, Henry (1750-1806), bookseller, Boston, Mass.
> Morris's Lecture on Architecture. 8 vols. ¶ *Catalogue* (1773), p. 26.

80. Morris, Robert (ca. 1702-54). *Select architecture: being regular designs of plans and elevations well suited to both town and country; in which the magnificence and beauty, the purity and simplicity of designing for every species of that noble art, is accurately treated, and with great variety exemplified, from the plain town-house to the stately hotel, and in the country from the genteel and convenient farm-house to the parochial church. With suitable embellishments. Also bridges, baths, summer-houses, &c. to all which such remarks, explanations and scales are annexed, that the comprehension is rendered easy, and subject most agreeable. Illustrated with fifty copper plates, quarto.* London, 1755. (29cm) Park 55

> Earlier edition published under the title: *Rural architecture: consisting of regular designs of plans and elevations for buildings in the country. In which the purity and simplicity of the art of designing are variously exemplified. With such remarks and explanations as are conducive to render the subject agreeable. Illustrated with fifty quarto copper-plates.*

London, 1750. (30cm)

Noel, Garrat (fl. 1752-75), bookseller, New York, N.Y.
 Morris's select Architecture. ¶ *Catalogue* (1762), p. 27.

Rivington, James (1724-1802), bookseller, New York, N.Y., & Philadelphia, Pa.
 Morris's select Architecture, being regular Designs for Town and Country Houses. ¶ *Catalogue* (1760), p. 46.

Rivington, James (1724-1802), & Samuel Brown (fl. 1755-69), booksellers, New York, N.Y., & Philadelphia, Pa.
 Morris select Architecture, being regular Designs for Town and Country Houses. ¶ *Catalogue* (1762), p. 67.

81. Morrison, Sir Richard (1767-1849). *Useful and ornamental designs in architecture, composed in the manner of the antique, and most approved taste of the present day, the whole being peculiarly adapted for execution.* Dublin, 1793. (folio)

Baltimore, Md., Library Company
 Morrison's Designs in Architecture. Folio. ¶ *Catalogue* (1798), p. 8.

Rice, Henry (d. 1804), & Patrick (fl. 1792-1804), booksellers, Philadelphia, Pa.
 Morreson's useful and ornamental designs in architecture, composed in the manner of the antique, and

most approved taste of the present day, the whole being peculiarly adapted for execution. Folio. ¶ *Catalogue* (1795), p. 60. Advertised for sale again in 1796.

82. Moxon, Joseph (1727-1700), tr. *The theory and practice of architecture; or Vitruvius and Vignola abridg'd. The first, by the famous Mr. Perrault, of the Royal Academy of Sciences in France, (and carefully done into English.) And the other by Joseph Moxon; and now accurately publish'd the fifth time.* Volume 2: *Vignola: or, the compleat architect. Shewing, in a plain and easy way, the rules of the five orders in architecture, viz. Tuscan, Dorick, Ionick, Corinthian and Composite. Whereby, any that can but read, and understand English, may readily learn the proportions that all members in a building have one unto another. Set forth by Mr. James Barazzio of Vignola. Translated into English, by Joseph Moxon. The fifth edition, with additions.* London 1702-03. 2 vols. (18cm)   Park 57

    Philadelphia, Pa., Loganian Library
        Vitruvius and Vignola abridged, the first by Mr. Perrault and the other by Jof. Moxon. London, 1703. Octavo. ¶ *Catalogue* (1760), p. 105.

83. [Neve, Richard (d. 1764)]. *The city and countrey purchaser, and builder's dictionary: or, the compleat builder's guide. Shewing the qualities, quantities, proportions, and rates or value of all materials relating to building; with the best method of preparing many of them. And also the customs, and methods of measuring of all artificers work, concern'd in building; together with the city and countrey prices, not only of workmanship, but of materials also: the which will be*

extraordinary useful in making of bargains, or contracts betwixt the workmaster and workman; and likewise in computing the value (or charge of erecting) of any fabrick, great or small. Likewise the explanation of the terms of art used by most workmen, together with aphorisms, or necessary rules in building, as to situation, contrivance, compactness, uniformity, conveniency, firmness, and form, &c. By T. N. Philomath. London, 1703. (19cm)   Park 58

Philadelphia, Pa., Association Library Company
    Builder's Dictionary, by Neave. Octavo. (Given to the library by William Williams) ¶ *A catalogue of books, belonging to the Association Library Company of Philadelphia* (Philadelphia: Bradford, 1765), p. 24.
                                                EAI: E10137; W51

Philadelphia, Pa., Library Company
    Neve's (Richard) City, Country-Purchasers, and Builder's Dictionary; or the complete Builder's Guide. Containing an explanation of all the terms of art used by workmen; as also what is necessary to be known in the art of building, as well by gentlemen as artificers of every denomination. 3d ed. London, 1736. Octavo. ¶ *Catalogue* (1770), n.p.

Philadelphia, Pa., Loganian Library
    Neve's, Rich. City and Country Purchaser and Builders Dictionary; shewing the Quantities, Rates, &c. of all Materials relating to Building, with the Explanation of the Terms of Art, and Rules in Building. London, 1726. Octavo. ¶ *Catalogue* (1760), p. 104.

Architectural Books in Early America

Philadelphia, Pa., Union Library Company
  Builders Dictionary: or, compleat Builders Guide; by Richard Neeve; the 3rd edition, improved. 1736. Octavo. ¶ *Catalogue* (1765), p. 5.

Yale College Library, New Haven, Conn.
  The Builder's Dictionary. ¶ *Catalogue* (1743), p. 43. Listed as *Neve's Builder's Dictionary* in 1791.

84. Nicholson, Peter (1765-1844). *The carpenter and joiner's assistant; containing practical rules for making all kinds of joints and various methods for hingeing them together; for hanging of doors on straight or circular plans; for fitting up windows and shutters to answer various purposes, with rules for hanging them: for the construction of floors, partitions, soffits, groins, arches for masonry; for constucting roofs in the best manner from a given quantity of timber: for placing of bond timbers; with various methods for adjusting raking pediments, enlarging and diminishing of mouldings; taking dimensions for joinery, and for setting out shop fronts. With a new scheme for constructing stairs and hand-rails, and for stairs having a conical well-hole, &c. &c. to which are added, examples of various roofs executed, with the scantlings, from actual measurements. With rules for mortices and tenons, and for fixing iron straps, &c. Also extracts from M. Belidor, M. du Hamel, M. de Buffon, &c. on the strength of timber, with practical observations. Illustrated with seventy-nine plates, and copious explanations.* London, [1792?]. (27cm)

Fenno, John Ward (1778-1802), bookseller, New York, N.Y.
  Nicholson's Carpenter's and Joiner's Assistant; containing practical rules for making all kinds of

joints, and various methods of hingeing them together, &c. 79 plates. Quarto. ¶ *Catalogue* (1800), p. 4.

85. Nicholson, Peter (1765-1844). *The carpenter's new guide: being a complete book of lines for carpentry and joinery. Treating fully on practical geometry, soffits, brick and plaister groins, niches of every description, sky-lights, lines for roofs and domes, with a great variety of designs for roofs, trussed girders, floors, domes, bridges, &c.;—stair-cases and hand-rails of various constructions; angle bars for shop fronts, &c.; and raking mouldings; with many other things entirely new. The whole founded on true geometrical principles; the theory and practice well explained, and fully exemplified on seventy-eight copper-plates, correctly engraved by the author. Including some observations and calculations on the strength of timber.* London, 1793. First American edition 1818. (28cm) Hitchcock 829-41

Thomas, Isaiah (1749-1831), Ebenezer Turrell Andrews (1766-1851), & Obadiah Penniman (1776-1820), booksellers, Albany, N.Y.
Carpenter's New Guide, by Peter Nicholson. ¶ *Catalogue* (1797?), p. 33.

White, James (1755?-1824), bookseller, Boston, Mass.
Nicholson's Carpenters New Guide. ¶ *Catalogue* (1797?), p. 21.

86. Nicholson, Peter (1765-1844). *The student's instructor in drawing and working the five orders of architecture. Fully explaining the best methods for striking regular and quirked mouldings; for diminishing and gluing of columns and*

capitals; for finding the true diameter of an order to any given height; for striking the Ionic volute, circular or elliptical; with finished examples, on a large scale, of the orders, their planceers, &c. and some designs for door-cases. Elegantly engraved on thirty-three plates. With explanations. London, 1795. First American edition 1837. (22cm)
Hitchcock 854

Fenno, John Ward (1778-1802), bookseller, New York, N.Y.
 Student's Instructor in drawing and working the Five Orders of Architecture, elegantly engraved on 33 plates, with explanations. Octavo. ¶ *Catalogue* (1800), p. [3].

Larkin, Ebenezer (1767-1813), bookseller, Boston, Mass.
 Architecture, Nicholson's. ¶ *Catalogue of books, for sale by E. Larkin* (Boston, 1798), p. 6.
EAI: E33982; W252

White, James (1755?-1824), bookseller, Boston, Mass.
 Nicholson's Students Instructor of Architecture. ¶ *Catalogue* (1797?), p. 21.

87. [Norman, John (1748?-1817), engr.]. *The town and country builder's assistant: absolutely necessary to be understood, by builders and workmen in general. Explaining short and easy rules. Made familiar to the meanest capacity, for drawing and working, I. The five orders of columns entire: or any part of an order, without regard to the module or diameter. And to enrich them with their rusticks, flutings, cablings, dentules, modillions, &t [sic]. Also to proportion their doors, windows, intercolumnations, portico's and arcades. Together with a*

variety of raking, circular, scrolled, compound, and contracted pedements; aud [sic] the true formation and accadering of their raking and returned cornices; and mouldings for capping their dentules and modillions. II. Block and cnataliver [sic] cornices, rustick quoins, cornices proportioned to rooms, or any height, angle brackets, mouldings for tabernacle frames, panneling, and centering for groins, trussed partitions, girders, roofs and dooms [sic]. Also the various methods of forming the heads of circular eliptical niches and buffets, the several kinds of staircases, to form the arch, or mould, to the hand-rail of a pair of stairs, which is the circular, part of the two first steps, so as to make it stand perpendicular over the ground, or plan, and the manner of squaring the rail without setting it up in its position. With pulpits, spires for steeples, chimney pieces, Chinese lattice-work for gates, pailings &c. The whole illustrated by upwards of 200 examples, engraved on 60 folio copper-plates. By a lover of architect. Boston, [1786]. (31.5cm)

Hitchcock 856-57

Beers, Isaac (1742?-1813), bookseller, New Haven, Conn.
  Town and Country Builder's Assistant. ¶ *Catalogue* (1791), p. 23.

Blake, William Pynson (1769-1820), bookseller, Boston, Mass.
  Town and Country Builder's Assistant. ¶ *Catalogue* (1793), p. 39. Advertised for sale again in 1796.

Blake, William Pynson (1769-1820), & Lemuel (1775-1861), booksellers, Boston, Mass.
  Town and Country Builder's Assistant. ¶ *Catalogue* (1798), p. 41.

Campbell, Robert (d. 1800), bookseller, Philadelphia, Pa.
The town and country builders assistant: absolutely necessary to be understood by builders and workmen in general, explaining short and easy rules made familiar to the meanest capacity for drawing working, &c. ¶ *Catalogue* (1791), pp. 35-36. Advertised for sale again in 1794, 1796, and 1797.

Campbell, Samuel (1763?-1836), bookseller, New York, N.Y.
The Town and Country Builder's Assistant, with copper-plates. Folio. ¶ *Catalogue* (1787), p. 27. Advertised for sale again in 1794 and 1799.

Carey, Mathew (1760-1839), bookseller, Philadelphia, Pa.
Pain's [sic] town and country builder's assistant, illustrated by upwards of 200 examples, engraved on 60 copperplates. Folio. ¶ *Catalogue* (1794), p. 61.

Guild, Benjamin (1749-92), bookseller, Boston, Mass.
Town and Country Builder's Assistant. Folio. ¶ *Catalogue* (1787; E22545), p. 24. Advertised for sale again in 1789 and 1790.

Larkin, Ebenezer (1767-1813), bookseller, Boston, Mass.
Town and Country Builder's Assistant. Folio. ¶ *Catalogue* (1793), p. 46.

Rice, Henry (d. 1804), & Patrick (fl. 1792-1804), booksellers, Philadelphia, Pa.
Town and country builder's assistant. Quarto. ¶ *Catalogue* (1795), p. 61. Advertised for sale again in 1796.

Spotswood, William (1753?-1805), bookseller, Boston, Mass., & Philadelphia, Pa.
 Town and country builder's assistant, absolutely necessary to be understood by builders and workmen in general. Illustrated by upwards of 200 examples, engraved on 60 folio copperplates. By a lover of architect. Folio. ¶ *Catalogue* (1795), p. 52.

Thomas, Isaiah (1749-1831), bookseller, Worcester, Mass., Boston, Mass., & Albany, N.Y.
 Town and Country Builder's Assistant. Folio. ¶ *Catalogue of books to be sold by Isaiah Thomas* (Worcester: Thomas, 1787), p. 17. Advertised for sale again in 1791 and 1792.   EAI: E20745; W121

Thomas, Isaiah (1749-1831), & Ebenezer Turrell Andrews (1766-1851), booksellers, Boston, Mass.
 Town and Country Builder's Assistant. Folio. ¶ *Catalogue* (1793), p. 47.

Thomas, Isaiah (1749-1831), Ebenezer Turrell Andrews (1766-1851), & Obadiah Penniman (1766-1820), booksellers, Albany, N.Y.
 Town and country Builders' Assistant. ¶ *Catalogue* (1797?), p. 34.

West, David (1765-1810), bookseller, Boston, Mass.
 Town and Country Builder's Assistant. Folio. ¶ *Catalogue* (1793), p. 47.

Young, William (1755-1829), bookseller, Philadelphia, Pa.
 Builders (The) Assistant, . . . Plates. Folio. ¶ *Books for sale* ([Philadelphia: Young, 1792]), p. 2.

EAI: E25062; W166

88. Oakley, Edward (d. 1756/66). *Every man a compleat builder: or, easy rules and proportions for drawing and working the several parts of architecture. Containing, I. Practical geometry. II. The five orders of architecture regulated by equal parts, with the manner of glewing up and fluting of columns and pilasters, after so concise a method, that renders it useful to all artists, and easy to every capacity. III. The method of reducing each order into practice, in the formation of designs for doors and windows. IV. Great variety of carpenter's work, shewing the method of placing girders, binding, bridging, and common joists, in flooring; various methods for scarfing together, raising plates, tenonting joists, and trussing girders, explaining a particular method of trussing a girder, when in its proper place, if any great weight should cause it to swag; the true method of finding the lengths and backings of hip rafters, for regular or irregular roofs. Trussed partitions and roofs, centerings for groins and angle brackets, demonstrated. V. Variety of plans, hand rails, newels, banisters and brackets for stair-cases; together with a true and concise method for striking the ramp and squaring the twisted rail, to square and circular plans. VI. The builder's dictionary, or, a practical and familiar explanation of the terms made use of in architecture, particularly describing the several parts and members contained in this book. The whole neatly engraved on 51 copper plates. Compiled by the late Edward Oakley, architect. To which is annexed, a plan, elevation, and section of the carpenter's work, erected to support the center-arch of Blackr-fryers-bridge.* London, 1766. First edition 1738. (22cm)   Park 59

Bradford, Thomas (1745-1838), bookseller, Philadelphia, Pa.
  Oakley's every man's complete builder. ¶ *Catalogue* (1796), p. 56.

89. Oakley, Edward (d. 1756/66). *The magazine of architecture, perspective, & sculpture: in five parts. Part the first, geometrical, practical, & usefull problems; for ye describing . . . of circles, ovals, arches, groyns (regular or rampant) & polygons, ye mouldings made use of in architecture; the handrail to stair-cases; ye wreath'd columns; ionic (capital antient & modern) volutes; & to flute columns, and pilasters. Part the second, plain & easy directions, for the construction of ye five orders of architecture, with their imposts & arches, plans, elevations & profiles, (accurately described by feet, inches & parts; likewise by the customary measure of modules & minutes) frontispieces & windows; ornaments for mouldings, capitals & freezes; fretts & flowers; enrich'd pedestals for statues; compartments for domes, soffits of arches & pavements; of the proportion and cieling of rooms; and designs of obelisks. Part the third, on the disposition & regularity of stair-cases; with several necessary improvements; wherein the symetry requir'd is preserv'd in ye steps & halfpaces, &c. also in ye rangeing ballisters & ornaments. Part the fourth, a most easy & expeditious method, to delineate in perspective; all designs relating to architecture, after a new manner, wholly free from ye confusion of occult lines. Part the fifth, the parts of human-body describ'd; with ye nature of motion reduc'd to geometrical rules; to which is added, a collection of ye most beautiful antique statues, with their parts describ'd, as measur'd from the originals. Engraven on 96 copper plates, by Benj:n Cole, to which is annex'd, an alphabetical explanation of ye terms made use of*

in architecture. Collected from the most approv'd authors, antient & modern; particularly, Palladio, Scamozzi & Vignola, & made a work of general use for gentlemen, architects, sculptors, painters, workmen, & all persons concern'd in building, by Edward Oakley, architect, M.M. Westminster, 1730. (37cm)   Park 60

Newport, R.I., Redwood Library
    Oakley's Magazine of Architecture, &c. Folio. ¶ *Catalogue* (1764), p. 5.

90. *Ornamental iron work, or designs in the present taste, for fan-lights, stair-case-railing, window-guard-irons, lamp-irons, palisades, & gates. With a scheme for adjusting designs with facility and accuracy to any slope. Engraved on twenty one plates.* London, [1800?]. (28cm)

Fenno, John Ward (1778-1802), bookseller, New York, N.Y.
    Ornamental Iron Work; or designs in the present taste for Fan Lights, Stair-case Railing, Window-guard Irons, Lamp Irons, Palisades and Gates, 21 plates. ¶ *Catalogue* (1800), p. 5.

91. *Ornaments displayed on a full-size for working. Proper for all carvers, painters, &c: containing a variety of accurate examples of foliage and friezes, on 33 folio plates.* London, [178-?]. (48cm)

Fenno, John Ward (1778-1802), bookseller, New York, N.Y.
    Ornaments Displayed, on a full size for working, proper for all Carvers, Painters, &c. containing a

Architectural Books in Early America

variety of accurate examples of Foilage and Friezes, on 33 folio plates. ¶ *Catalogue* (1800), p. 5.

92. Over, Charles. *Ornamental architecture, in the Gothic, Chinese and modern taste, being above fifty intire new designs of plans, sections, elevations, &c. (many of which may be executed with roots of trees) for gardens, parks, forests, woods, canals, &c. containing paling of several sorts, gates, garden seats, both close and open, umbrello's, alcoves, grotto's and grotesque seats, hermitages, triumphal arches, temples, banqueting houses and rooms, rotundo's, observatories, ice-houses, bridges, boats, and cascades. Also, an obelisk or monument, with directions where proper to be erected, and the method how to execute them. The whole neatly engrav'd on fifty four copper-plates. From the designs of Charles Over, architect.* London, 1758. (21cm)   Park 61

    Bell, Robert (1731?-84), bookseller, Philadelphia, Pa.
        Over's Ornamental Architecture, being 50 New Designs of Plans, Sections, Elevations, &c. ¶ *Catalogue* (1783), p. 60.

    Noel, Garrat (fl. 1752-75), bookseller, New York, N.Y.
        Over's Ornamental Architecture. ¶ *Catalogue* (1762), p. 27.

    Noel, Garrat (fl. 1752-75), & Ebenezer Hazard (1744-1817), booksellers, New York, N.Y.
        Over's Ornamental Architecture. ¶ *Catalogue* (1771), p. 18.

    Rivington, James (1724-1802), bookseller, New York, N.Y., & Philadelphia, Pa.

Over's Ornamental Architecture, in the Gothic, Chinese and Modern Taste. ¶ *Catalogue* (1760), p. 46.

Rivington, James (1724-1802), & Samuel Brown (fl. 1755-69), booksellers, New York, N.Y., & Philadelphia, Pa.
Over's Ornamental Architecture, in the Gothic, Chinese and Modern Taste. ¶ *Catalogue* (1762), p. 68.

93. Pain, William (1730?-90?). *The builder's companion, and workman's general assistant: demonstrating, after the most easy and practical method, all the principal rules of architecture, from the plan to the ornamental finish; illustrated with a great number of useful and familiar examples than any work of that kind hitherto published; with clear and ample instructions, annexed to each subject or number, on the same plate; being not only useful but necessary to all masons, bricklayers, plasterers, carpenters, joiners, and others concerned in the several branches of building, &c. Also the figure, description, and use of a new-invented joint-rule; so calculated as to render easy the drawing of any figure, architrave, frize, cornice, or moulding, that can be required to any given scale. The whole correctly engraven on seventy-seven folio copper-plates from the designs of William Pain.* London, 1758. (36cm)   Park 63

Blake, William Pynson (1769-1820), bookseller, Boston, Mass.
Paine's Builder's Companion. ¶ *Catalogue* (1793), p. 31. Advertised for sale again in 1796.

Boston, Mass., broadside, September 30, 1766
    Paine's Builder's Companion. Folio. ¶ *Catalogue* (1766), broadside.

Charleston, S.C., Library Society
    Pain's builder's companion. London, 1765. Folio. ¶ *Catalogue* (1770), p. 9.

Hall, David (1714-74), bookseller, Philadelphia, Pa.
    The builder's companion. ¶ *Catalogue* (1763?), broadsheet.

Knox, Henry (1750-1806), bookseller, Boston, Mass.
    Paine's Companion and Workmans general Assistant. Folio. ¶ *Catalogue* (1773), p. 29.

Noel, Garrat (fl. 1752-75), bookseller, New York, N.Y.
    Paine's Builder's Companion. ¶ *Catalogue* (1762), p. 27.

Noel, Garrat (fl. 1752-75), & Ebenezer Hazard (1744-1817), booksellers, New York, N.Y.
    Pain's Builder's Companion. ¶ *Catalogue* (1771), p. 18.

Rivington, James (1724-1802), bookseller, New York, N.Y., & Philadelphia, Pa.
    The Builder's Companion or Workman's general Assistant, demonstrating all the principal Rules of Architecture, from the Plan to the Finish of the Work, with clear Instructions annexed to each Subject, useful to all Masons, Bricklayers, Plaisterers, Carpenters, Joyners, and all concerned in the various

Branches of Building, with 77 Copper Plates. By William Pain. ¶ *Catalogue* (1760), pp. 45-46.

Rivington, James (1724-1802), & Samuel Brown (fl. 1755-69), booksellers, New York, N.Y., & Philadelphia, Pa.
The Builder's Companion or Workman's general Assistant, demonstrating all the principal Rules of Architecture, from the Plan to the Finish of the Work, with clear Instructions annexed to each Subject, useful to all Masons, Bricklayers, Plaisterers, Carpenters, Joyners, and all concerned in the various Branches of Building, with 77 Copper Plates. By William Pain. ¶ *Catalogue* (1762), p. 67.

94. Pain, William (1730?-90?). *The builder's pocket-treasure; or Palladio delineated and explained, in such a manner as to render that most excellent author plain and intelligible to the meanest capacity, in which not only the theory, but the practical part of architecture has been carefully attended to. Illustrated with new and useful designs of frontispieces, chimney-pieces, &c. with their bases, capitals, and entablatures, at large for practice; architrave frontispieces, cornices, and mouldings for the inside of rooms, &c. the construction of stairs, with their ramp and twist rails; framing of floors, roofs, and partitions; with the method of finding the length and backing of hips, streight or curvi-linear; the tracing of groins, angle-brackets, splay'd or circular soffits; with plans and elevations of a dwelling-house, hot-house, garden temple, seat and bridge; and a table of scantlings for cutting timber for building. The whole neatly and correctly engraved on forty-four copper plates, with printed explanations to face each plate.* London, 1763. First American edition 1794.

(18.5cm) Park 64; Hitchcock 894

Blake, William Pynson (1769-1820), bookseller, Boston, Mass.
 Paine's Builder's Treasure. ¶ *Catalogue* (1793), p. 31.

Blake, William Pynson (1769-1820), & Lemuel (1775-1861), booksellers, Boston, Mass.
 Paine's Builder's Pocket Treasure. ¶ *Catalogue* (1798), p. 33.

Campbell, Robert (d. 1800), bookseller, Philadelphia, Pa.
 Pain's Builders pocket-treasure. Quarto. ¶ *Robert Campbell and Co's. catalogue for 1797* (Philadelphia, 1797), p. 58. EAI: E31913; W234

Campbell, Samuel (1763?-1836), bookseller, New York, N.Y.
 Pain's Builder's Pocket Treasure. Octavo. ¶ *Catalogue* (1798), p. 25.

Fenno, John Ward (1778-1802), bookseller, New York, N.Y.
 Builder's Pocket Treasure, in which not only the theory but the practical parts of Architecture are carefully explained, 55 plates. Octavo. ¶ *Catalogue* (1800), p. 6.

Guild, Benjamin (1749-92), bookseller, Boston, Mass.
 Paine's Builder's Treasure. ¶ *New select catalogue of Benjamin Guild's Circulating Library* (Boston, 1789), p. 25. EAI: E21868; W129

Hanover, N.H., Hanover Bookstore
   Pain's Builder's Pocket Treasure, correctly Engraved on 55 Plates, with explanations. ¶ *Catalogue* (1799), p. 21.

Knox, Henry (1750-1806), bookseller, Boston, Mass.
   Paine's Builder's Treasure. Octavo. ¶ *Catalogue* (1773), p. 29.

Larkin, Ebenezer (1767-1813), bookseller, Boston, Mass.
   Pain's Builder's Pocket Treasure, correctly engraved on 55 Plates, with Explanations. ¶ *Catalogue* (1798), p. 38.

Larkin, Samuel (1773-1849), bookseller, Portsmouth, N.H.
   Paine's Builder's Pocket Treasure. ¶ *A catalogue of books, for sale or circulation* (Portsmouth, 1796), p. 18.
   EAI: E30672; W217

Thomas, Isaiah (1749-1831), & Ebenezer Turrell Andrews (1766-1851), booksellers, Boston, Mass.
   Pain's Builder's Pocket Treasure, correctly Engraved on 55 Plates, with explanations. ¶ *Catalogue* (1799), p. 23.

Thomas, Isaiah (1749-1831), Ebenezer Turell Andrews (1766-1851), & Obadiah Penniman (1776-1820), booksellers, Albany, N.Y.
   Paine's Builder's Pocket Treasure. ¶ *American publications. Catalogue of books, for sale, wholesale or retail, at the bookstore of Thomas, Andrews & Penniman, Albany* ([Albany: Barber & Southwick, 1796]), broad-

side. Advertised for sale again in 1797.
EAI: E31293; W226

Thomas, Isaiah (1749-1831), Isaiah Thomas, Jr. (1773-1819), & Alexander Thomas (1775-1809), booksellers, Worcester, Mass.
Paine's Pocket Treasure, with elegant designs. Duodecimo. ¶ *Catalogue* (1796), p. 37.

West, David (1765-1810), bookseller, Boston, Mass.
Pain's (William) Builder's Pocket Treasure, correctly Engraved on 55 Plates, with explanations. ¶ *Catalogue* (1799), p. 22.

West, John (1770-1827), bookseller, Boston, Mass.
Pain's (William) Builder's Pocket Treasure, correctly Engraven on 55 Plates, with explanations. ¶ *A catalogue of books published in America, and for sale at the bookstore of John West* (Boston: Etheridge, 1797), p. 23.
EAI: E33205; W246

White, James (1755?-1824), bookseller, Boston, Mass.
Pain's Pocket Treasure. ¶ *Catalogue* (1797?), p. 23.

95. Pain, William (1730?-90?). *The carpenter's and joiner's repository; or, a new system of lines and proportions for doors, windows, chimnies, cornices, and mouldings, for finishing rooms, &c. &c. A great variety of stair-cases, on a plan entirely new, and easy to be understood. Circular circular soffits, flewing and winding, in straight and circular walls, groins, angle-brackets, circular and elliptical sky-lights, and the method of squaring and preparing their circular bars, shop-fronts, &c. . . . Engraved on sixty-nine copper-plates.*

London, 1778. (37.5cm)

Baltimore, Md., Library Company
 Pain's Carpenter's and Joiner's Repository. Folio. ¶ *Catalogue* (1798), p. 8.

Fenno, John Ward (1778-1802), bookseller, New York, N.Y.
 Carpenter's and Joiner's Repository; or a new system of lines and proportions for doors, windows, &c. a great variety of stair-cases, on a plan entirely new, by Wm. Pain. New edition, . . . 69 plates. Folio. ¶ *Catalogue* (1800), p. 4.

Guild, Benjamin (1749-92), bookseller, Boston, Mass.
 Paine's System of Architecture. Folio. ¶ *Catalogue* (1787?; E22545), p. 19.

New York, N.Y., Society Library
 Pain's (W.) carpenters and joiners repository, engraved on sixty-nine copperplates. Folio. ¶ *Catalogue* (1791), p. 98.

96. Pain, William (1730?-90?). *The carpenter's pocket directory; containing the best methods of framing timber buildings of all figures and dimensions, with their several parts, as floors, roofs in ledgment, their lengths and backings; trussed roofs, spires, and domes; trussing-girders, partitions, and bridges, with abutments; centering for arches, vaults, &c. cutting stone ceilings, groins, &c. with their moulds; centers for drawing Gothic arches, ellipses, &c. &c. With the plan and sections of a barn. Engraved on twenty-four plates, with explanations, forming the most complete and useful work of the kind yet*

published. London, 1781. First American edition 1797. (20cm)   Hitchcock 895

Blake, William Pynson (1769-1820), & Lemuel (1775-1861), booksellers, Boston, Mass.
    Paine's Carpenter's Pocket Directory. ¶ *Catalogue* (1798), p. 33.

Carey, Mathew (1760-1839), bookseller, Philadelphia, Pa.
    Carpenter's Directory. ¶ *Philadelphia, June 23, 1798. Mathew Carey's exchange catalogue* ([Philadelphia: Carey, 1798]), broadside.   EAI: E33497; W250

Fenno, John Ward (1778-1802), bookseller, New York, N.Y.
    Carpenter's Pocket Directory, containing the best method of framing timber buildings, &c. a new edition. Quarto. ¶ *Catalogue* (1800), p. [3].

Hudson, Barzillai (1741-1823), & George Goodwin (1757-1844), booksellers, Hartford, Conn.
    Paine's Carpenter's Pocket Directory. ¶ *Hudson & Goodwin, have for sale . . . the following books* ([Hartford: Hudson & Goodwin, 1797]), broadside.
                                        EAI: E48154: W238

Larkin, Ebenezer (1767-1813), bookseller, Boston, Mass.
    Pain's (William) Pocket Directory. Quarto. ¶ *Catalogue* (1793), p. 46.

Thomas, Isaiah (1749-1831), bookseller, Worcester, Mass., Boston, Mass., & Albany, N.Y.
    Carpenter's Pocket Dictionary. ¶ *Catalogue* (1787),

p. 17.

Thomas, Isaiah (1749-1831), & Ebenezer Turrell Andrews (1766-1851), booksellers, Boston, Mass.
 Pain's (William) Pocket Directory. Quarto. ¶ *Catalogue* (1793), p. 47.

Thomas, Isaiah (1749-1831), Ebenezer Turrell Andrews, & Obadiah Penniman (1776-1820), booksellers, Albany, N.Y.
 Paine's Pocket Directory. Quarto. ¶ *Catalogue* (1797?), p. 33.

West, David (1765-1810), bookseller, Boston, Mass.
 Pain's (William) Pocket Directory. Quarto. ¶ *Catalogue* (1793), p. 47.

White, James (1755-1824), bookseller, Boston, Mass.
 Pain's Carpenters Pocket Dictionary. ¶ *Catalogue* (1797?), p. 23.

97. Pain, William (1730?-90?). *Pain's British Palladio or, the builder's general assistant. Demonstrating, in the most easy and practical method, all the principal rules of architecture, from the ground plan to the ornamental finish. Illustrated with several new and useful designs of houses, with their plans, elevations, and sections. Also, clear and ample instructions, annexed to each subject, in letter-press; with a list of prices for materials and labour, and labour only. This work will be universally useful to all carpenters, bricklayers, masons, joiners, plaisterers, and others, concerned in the several branches of building, &c. comprehending the following subjects, viz. Plans, elevations, and sections, of*

gentlemen's houses. Designs for doors, chimneys, and ceilings, with their proper embellishments, in the most modern taste. A great variety of mouldings, for base and surbase architraves, imposts, friezes, and cornices, with their proper ornaments, for practice, drawn to half-size: to which are added, scales for enlarging or lessening at pleasure, if required. Also, great variety of stair-cases; shewing the practical method of executing them, in any case required, viz. groins, angle-brackets, circular circular flewing and winding soffits, domes, sky-lights, &c. all made plain and easy to the meanest capacity. The proportion of windows for the light to rooms. Preparing foundations; the proportion of chimneys to rooms, and sections of flews. The principal timbers properly laid out on each plan, viz. the manner of framing the roofs, and finding the length and backing of hips, either square or bevel. Scantlings of the timbers, figured in proportion to their bearing. The method for trussing girders, scarfing plates, &c. And many other articles, particularly useful to all persons in the building profession. The whole correctly engraved on forty-two folio copper-plates, from the original designs of William and James Pain. London, 1786. (43cm)

Baltimore, Md., Library Company
    Pain's British Palladio, (Plates). Folio. ¶ *Catalogue* (1797), p. 7.

Fenno, John Ward (1778-1802), bookseller, New York, N.Y.
    Pain's British Palladio; or the Builder's General Assistant: demonstrating in the most easy and practical method, all the principal rules of Architecture, illustrated with 42 copper-plates. Folio. ¶ *Catalogue* (1800), p. 5.

Hudson, Barzillai (1741-1823), & George Goodwin (1757-1844), booksellers, Hartford, Conn.
 Paine's British Palladio. ¶ *Catalogue* (1797), broadside.

Larkin, Ebenezer (1767-1813), bookseller, Boston, Mass.
 Pain's (William) British Palladio. Folio. ¶ *Catalogue* (1793), p. 46.

Larkin, Samuel (1773-1849), bookseller, Portsmouth, N.H.
 Paine's British Palladio. ¶ *Catalogue* (1796), p. 18.

Philadelphia, Pa., Library Company
 Pain's (William and James) British palladio; or, the builder's general assistant. Demonstrating all the principal rules of architecture, from the ground plan to the ornamental finish; with plates. London, 1790. Folio. ¶ *Catalogue* (1794), p. 4.

Thomas, Isaiah (1749-1831), & Ebenezer Turrell Andrews (1766-1851), booksellers, Boston, Mass.
 Pain's (William) British Palladio. Folio. ¶ *Catalogue* (1793), p. 47.

Thomas, Isaiah (1749-1831), Ebenezer Turrell Andrews (1766-1851), & Obadiah Penniman (1776-1820), booksellers, Albany, N.Y.
 Paine's British Palladio. Folio. ¶ *Catalogue* (1797?), p. 33.

West, David (1765-1810), bookseller, Boston, Mass.
 Pain's (William) British Palladio. Folio. ¶ *Catalogue*

Architectural Books in Early America

(1793), p. 47.

White, James (1755?-1824), bookseller, Boston, Mass.
Pain's Palladio, or Builders General Assistant. ¶ *Catalogue* (1797?), p. 23.

98. Pain, William (1730?-90?). *The practical builder, or workman's general assistant: shewing the most approved and easy methods for drawing and working the whole or separate part of any building, as the use of the tramel for groins, anglebrackets, niches, &c. semi-circular arches on flewing jambs, the preparing and making their soffits. Rules of carpentry; to find the length and backing of hips, strait or curved; trusses for roofs, domes, &c.—Trussing of girders, sections of floors, &c. The proportion of the five orders, in their general and particular parts, gluing of columns, stair-cases with their ramp and twist rails, fixing the carriages, newels, &c. Frontispieces, chimney-pieces, ceilings, cornices, architraves, &c. in the newest taste. With plans and elevations of gentlemens and farm-houses, yards, barns, &c. . . . Engraved on eighty-three plates.* London, 1774. First American edition 1792. (27.5cm) Hitchcock 896

Blake, William Pynson (1769-1820), bookseller, Boston, Mass.
    Paine's Practical Builder. ¶ *Catalogue* (1793), p. 31. Advertised for sale again in 1796.

Blake, William Pynson (1769-1820), & Lemuel (1775-1861), booksellers, Boston, Mass.
    Paine's Practical Builder. ¶ *Catalogue* (1798), p. 33.

Campbell, Robert (d. 1800), bookseller, Philadelphia, Pa.

Paine's practical builder, or workman's general assistant. ¶ *Robert Campbell's catalogue of books* (Philadelphia: [R. Campbell], Sept. 13, 1794), p. 54. Advertised for sale again in 1796 and 1797.
EAI: E26727; W183

Campbell, Samuel (1763?-1836), bookseller, New York, N.Y.
Pain's practical builder, engraved on 83 plates. Boston, 1792. Quarto. ¶ *Catalogue* (1794), p. 32. Advertised for sale again in 1799.

Carey, Mathew (1760-1839), bookseller, Philadelphia, Pa.
Pain's practical builder, or workman's general assistant, illustrated by 83 copperplates. Quarto. ¶ *Catalogue* (1794), p. 61.

Dabney, John (1752-1819), bookseller, Salem, Mass.
Paine's Practical Builder. ¶ *Catalogue* (1794), p. 24.

Fenno, John Ward (1778-1802), bookseller, New York, N.Y.
Pain's practical Builder, or Workman's General Assistant; shewing the most approved methods for drawing and working the whole or separate part of any building. 83 plates. Quarto. ¶ *Catalogue* (1800), p. 4.

Hanover, N.H., Hanover Bookstore
Pain's (William) Practical Builder; or, Workman's general Assistant, engraved on 83 Plates, with explanations. Quarto. ¶ *Catalogue* (1799), p. 21.

Larkin, Ebenezer (1767-1813), bookseller, Boston, Mass.
Pain's (William) Practical Builder. Quarto. ¶ *Catalogue* (1793), p. 46. Advertised for sale again in 1798.

Larkin, Samuel (1773-1849), bookseller, Portsmouth, N.H.
Paine's Practical Builder. ¶ *Catalogue* (1796), p. 18.

Nancrede, Paul Joseph Guérard de (1760-1841), bookseller, Boston, Mass.
Pain's practical builder. Quarto. ¶ *Catalogue* (1796), p. 23. Advertised for sale again in 1798.

Rice, Henry (d. 1804), & Patrick (fl. 1792-1804), booksellers, Philadelphia, Pa.
Pain's practical builder, or workman's general assistant. Quarto. ¶ *Catalogue* (1795), p. 60. Advertised for sale again in 1796.

Spotswood, William (1753?-1805), bookseller, Boston, Mass., & Philadelphia, Pa.
Practical builder; or, workman's general assistant. Showing the most approved and easy methods for drawing and working the whole or separate part of any building. By William Pain, architect and joiner. Engraved on 83 plates. Quarto. ¶ *Catalogue* (1795), p. 52.

Thomas, Isaiah (1749-1831), bookseller, Worcester, Mass., Boston, Mass., & Albany, N.Y.
Paine's Practical Builder, with elegant Designs. Quarto. ¶ *Catalogue* (1792), p. 31.

Thomas, Isaiah (1749-1831), & Ebenezer Turrell Andrews (1766-1851), booksellers, Boston, Mass.
>Pain's (William) Practical Builder. Quarto. ¶ *Catalogue* (1793), p. 47. Advertised for sale again in 1799.

Thomas, Isaiah (1749-1831), Ebenezer Turrell Andrews (1766-1851), & Obadiah Penniman (1776-1820), booksellers, Albany, N.Y.
>Paine's Practical Builder. ¶ *Catalogue* (1796), broadside. Advertised for sale again in 1797.

Thomas, Isaiah (1749-1831), Isaiah Thomas, Jr. (1773-1819), & Alexander Thomas (1775-1809), booksellers, Worcester, Mass.
>Paine's Practical Builder, with elegant designs. Quarto. ¶ *Catalogue* (1796), p. 37.

West, David (1765-1810), bookseller, Boston, Mass.
>Pain's (William) Practical Builder. Quarto. ¶ *Catalogue* (1793), p. 47. Advertised for sale again in 1799.

West, John (1770-1827), bookseller, Boston, Mass.
>Pain's (William) Practical Builder, or, Workman's General Assistant, engraved on 83 Plates, with explanations. ¶ *Catalogue* (1797), p. 23.

White, James (1755?-1824), bookseller, Boston, Mass.
>Pain's Practical Builder. ¶ *Catalogue* (1797?), p. 23.

99. Pain, William (1730?-90?). *The practical house carpenter; or, the youth's instructor: containing a great variety of mouldings at large for practice, with their proper embellishments, two designs for gentlemen's houses, with their plans, eleva-*

tions, and sections; likewise, a great variety of stair-case work, laid down to a very large scale for practice. To which is added, a treatise on Gothic architecture, with columns, entablatures, frontispieces, chimney pieces, shop fronts, cielings, &c. A plan and elevation of a Gothic temple, and a plan and elevation of a gentleman's house in the Gothic taste. All laid down in a plain and practical manner for practice. Engraved on thirty-four folio copper plates. By William Pain. . . . The second edition, with additions. London, 1788. First American edition 1796. (22.5cm) Hitchcock 897-98

Blake, William Pynson (1769-1820), & Lemuel (1775-1861), booksellers, Boston, Mass.
 Paine's Practical House Carpenter. ¶ *Catalogue* (1798), p. 33.

Bristol, R.I., Potter Library Company
 Pain's House Carpenter. ¶ *The by-laws and catalogue of the Potter Library Company* (Warren, R.I.: Phillips, 1800), p. 21. EAI: E37049; W283

Fenno, John Ward (1778-1802), bookseller, New York, N.Y.
 The Practical House-Carpenter; or Youth's Instructor, by Wm. Pain: containing a great variety of useful designs in Carpentry and Architecture: the whole illustrated and made perfectly easy by 148 copperplates. Quarto. ¶ *Catalogue* (1800), p. [3].

Hanover, N.H., Hanover Bookstore
 Pain's Practical House Carpenter, engraved on 148 copperplates, with explanations to each. Quarto. ¶ *Catalogue* (1799), p. 21.

Larkin, Samuel (1773-1849), bookseller, Portsmouth, N.H.
Paine's Practical House Carpenter. ¶ *Catalogue* (1796), p. 18.

Nancrede, Paul Joseph Guérard de (1760-1841), bookseller, Boston, Mass.
House carpenter, . . . by Pain. Quarto. ¶ *Catalogue* (1796), p. 16.

Thomas, Isaiah (1749-1831), & Ebenezer Turrell Andrews (1766-1851), booksellers, Boston, Mass.
Pain's Practical House Carpenter, engraved on 148 copperplates, with explanations to each. Quarto. ¶ *Catalogue* (1799), p. 23.

Thomas, Isaiah (1749-1831), Ebenezer Turrell Andrews (1766-1851), & Obadiah Penniman (1776-1820), booksellers, Albany, N.Y.
Painc's Practical House Carpenter. Quarto. ¶ *Catalogue* (1797?), p. 33.

West, David (1765-1810), bookseller, Boston, Mass.
Pain's Practical House Carpenter, engraved on 148 copperplates, with explanations to each. Quarto. ¶ *Catalogue* (1799), p. 23.

White, James (1755?-1824), bookseller, Boston, Mass.
Pain's House Carpenter. ¶ *Catalogue* (1797?), p. 23.

100. Paine, James (1717-89). *Plans, elevations and sections of noblemen and gentlemen's houses, and also of stabling, bridges, public and private, temples, and other garden*

Architectural Books in Early America

buildings; executed in the counties of Derby, Durham, Middlesex, Northumberland, Nottingham, and York.... Part the first. Illustrated by seventy-four large folio plates. Volume 2: Plans, elevations, and sections, of noblemen and gentlemen's houses, and also of bridges, public and private, temples, and other garden buildings; executed in the counties of Nottingham, Essex, Wilts, Derby, Hertford, Suffolk, Salop, Middlesex, and Surrey.... Part the second. Illustrated by one hundred and one large folio plates.* 2 vols. London, 1767-83. (53cm)

Baltimore, Md., Library Company
    Pain's Plans, Elevations, Sections, &c. 2 vols. Folio. ¶ *Catalogue* (1797), p. 7.

101. Palladio, Andrea (1508-80). *I quattro libri dell'architettura di Andrea Palladio. Ne' quali, dopo un breue trattato de' cinque ordini, & di quelli auertimenti, che sono piu necessarij nel fabricare; si tratta delle case private, delle vie, de i ponti, delle piazze, de i xisti, et de' tempij.* Venetia, 1570. (31cm)   Park 65

    Harvard College Library, Cambridge, Mass.
        Palladio (Andr.) Del l'architettura. Venetia, 1570. Folio. ¶ *Catalogue* (1790), p. 8. Identified by Park as being in the Harvard College Library in 1765. According to Dr. Frank H. Sommer, the 1570 edition given by Thomas Hollis to Harvard was an eighteenth-century edition of Palladio's publication with line engravings in place of the original woodcut illustrations.

    Palladio (Andr.) Del l'architettura. Venetia, 1581.

Folio. ¶ *Catalogue,* (1790), p. 8. Identified by Park as being in the Harvard College Library in 1765.

102. [Peacock, James (1738?-1814)]. Οἰκίδια, *or, nutshells: being ichnographic distributions for small villas; chiefly upon oeconomical principles. In seven classes. With occasional remarks. By Jose Mac Packe, a bricklayer's labourer. Part the first, containing twelve designs.* London, 1785. (21.5cm)

Baltimore, Md., Library Company
   Nutshells; or Ichnographic Distribution of small Villas. Octavo. ¶ *Catalogue* (1798), p. 10.

Hudson, Barzillai (1741-1823), & George Goodwin (1757-1844), booksellers, Hartford, Conn.
   Nutshell's Plans of Houses. ¶ *Catalogue* (1797), broadside.

Philadelphia, Pa., Library Company
   Oikidia; or nutshells; being ichnographic distributions for small villas; chiefly upon oeconomical principles; with plates. London, 1785. Octavo. ¶ *Catalogue* (1789), p. 254.

103. Perrault, Charles (1628-1703). *Parallele des anciens et des moderns en ce qui regarde les arts et les sciences.* Part 2 of volume 1 has the title: *Parallele des anciens et des modernes en ce qui regarde l'architecture, la sculpture, et la peinture: second dialogue.* 4 vols. Paris, 1688-97. (17cm)

Philadelphia, Pa., Loganian Library
   Perrault, Paralele des Anciens et des moderns en

[c]e qui regarde les arts et les Sciences. Paris, 1693. ¶ *Catalogue* (1795), p. 166.

104. Perrault, Claude (1613-88). *Architecture générale de Vitruve, réduit en abrégé, par Mr. Perrault de l'Academie des Sciences à Paris. Denière édition enrichie de figures en cuivres.* Amsterdam, 1681. (16cm)

    Bell, Robert (1731?-84), bookseller, Philadelphia, Pa. Architecture Generale de Vitrove. ¶ *Catalogue* (1783), p. 11.

105. Perrault, Claude (1613-88). *Ordonnance des cinq espèces de colonnes selon la méthode des anciens.* Paris, 1683. (37.5cm) Park 66

    A treatise of the five orders of columns in architecture, viz. Toscan, Doric, Ionic, Corinthian and Composite. Wherein the proportions and characters of the members of their several pedestals, columns and entablatures, are distinctly consider'd, with respect to the practice of the antients and moderns. Also a most natural, easie and practicable method laid down, for determining the most minute part in all the orders, without a fraction. To which is annex'd, a discourse concerning pilasters: and of several abuses introduc'd into architecture. Engraven on six folio plates of the several orders, adorn'd with twenty-four borders, as many initial letters, and a like number of tail-pieces, by John Sturt. Written in French by Claude Perrault, ... Made English by John James of Greenwich. London, 1708. (37cm)

    Park 66

    Harvard College Library, Cambridge, Mass.

Perrault (Claud.) Treatise of the five Orders of Columns in Architecture. London, 1708. Folio. ¶ *Catalogue* (1723), p. 27.

Philadelphia, Pa., Library Company
Perrault's (Claude) Treatise of the five Orders of Columns, in Architecture: wherein the proportions and characters of the members of their several pedestals, columns, and entablatures are distinctly considered, with respect to the practice of the antients and moderns. Also a most natural, easy, and practicable method laid down, for determining the most minute part in all the orders, without a fraction. To which is annexed, a discourse concerning pilasters. Translated from the French, by John James. London, 1708. Folio. ¶ *Catalogue* (1770), n.p.

Philadelphia, Pa., Union Library Company
A Treatise of the Five Orders of Columns in Architecture, viz Toscan, Doric, Ionic, Corinthian, and Composite. Wherein the Proportions and Characters of the Members of their several Pedestals, Columns, and Entabletures, are distinctly considered with Respect of the Antients and Moderns. Also, a most natural easy and practicable Method laid down for determining the most minute Part in all the Orders, without a Fraction. To which is annexed, A Discourse concerning Pilasters, and of several Abuses introduced into Architecture. Engraven on Six Folio Plates of the several Orders, adorned with 24 Borders, as many initial Letters, and a like Number of Tail Pieces.

By John Stuart. Written in French by Claude Perrault, of the Royal Academy of Paris. Made English by John James, of Greenwich. London, 1708. Folio. ¶ *A catalogue of books belonging to the Union-Library-Company of Philadelphia* (Philadelphia: Chattin, 1754), p. 28.   EAI: E7295; W24

106. Plaw, John (ca. 1745-1820). *Ferme ornée; or rural improvements. A series of domestic and ornamental designs, suited to parks, plantations, rides, walks, rivers, farms, &c. Consisting of fences, paddock houses, a bath, a dog-kennel, pavilions, farm-yards, fishing-houses, sporting-boxes, shooting-lodges, single and double cottages, &c. calculated for landscape and picturesque effects. Engraved on thirty-eight plates. With appropriate scenery, plans, and explanations.* London, 1795. (31cm)

Philadelphia, Pa., Library Company
Plaw's Ferme Ornée; or, rural improvements. A series of domestic and ornamental designs, suited to parks, plantations, &c. with plates. London, 1796. Quarto. ¶ *Fourth supplement to the catalogue of books, belonging to the Library Company of Philadelphia* (Philadelphia: Poulson, 1798), p. 8.
EAI: E34357; W254

107. Plaw, John (ca. 1745-1820). *Sketches for country houses, villas, and rural dwellings; calculated for persons of moderate income, and for comfortable retirement. Also some designs for cottages, which may be constructed of the simplest materials; with plans and general estimates.* London, 1800. (32cm)

Architectural Books in Early America

Fenno, John Ward (1778-1802), bookseller, New York, N.Y.
> Plaw's Cottages; or sketches for Country-houses, Villas, and Rural Dwellings; calculated for persons of moderate income, and for comfortable retirement, . . . 41 plates in aqua tinta. Quarto. ¶ *Catalogue* (1800), pp. 4-5.

108. Pool, Robert, & John Cash. *Views of the most remarkable public buildings, monuments and other edifices in the city of Dublin, delineated by Robert Pool and John Cash with historical descriptions of each building. Patronized by the Dublin Society.* Dublin, 1780. (24cm)

Carey, Mathew (1760-1839), bookseller, Philadelphia, Pa.
> Pool and Cash's view of the most remarkable public buildings, monuments, and edifices in the city of Dublin. Quarto. ¶ *Catalogue* (1794), p. 61.

Ross, Joseph, & George Douglas, booksellers, Petersburgh, Va.
> Views of the most remarkable Buildings in the City of Dublin, beautifully engraved, with Descriptions. Quarto. ¶ *Catalogue* (1800), p. 29.

109. Price, Francis (ca. 1704-53). *The British carpenter: or, a treatise on carpentry. Containing the most concise and authentick rules of that art, in a more useful and extensive method, than has been made publick. The second edition enlarged, with an addition of sixteen copper-plates.* London, 1735. Bound with: *A supplement to the British carpenter: containing Palladio's orders of architecture, with*

the ornaments of doors and windows, proportion'd and adjusted by divisions on scales; together with the accurate curves of their mouldings, and their application to use. Described on sixteen copper-plates. London, 1735. First edition 1733. (26cm)   Park 67

Allen, Thomas (fl. 1785-1799), bookseller, New York, N.Y.
    Price's British Carpenter. Quarto. ¶ *Catalogue* (1792), p. 26.

Baltimore, Md., Library Company
    Price's British Carpenter. Quarto. ¶ *Catalogue* (1798), p. 9.

Beers, Isaac (1742?-1813), bookseller, New Haven, Conn.
    Price's British Carpenter. ¶ *Catalogue* (1791), p. 23.

Campbell, Samuel (1763?-1836), bookseller, New York, N.Y.
    Prices' British Carpenters Instructor, with copper-plates. Quarto. ¶ *Catalogue* (1787), p. 27.

Caritat, Louis Alexis Hocquet de (b. 1752), bookseller, New York, N.Y.
    Price's British Carpenter. ¶ *Catalogue* (1799), p. 80.

Charleston, S.C., Library Society
    Price's British carpenter. London, 1735. Quarto. ¶ *Catalogue* (1770), p. 14.

Dunlap, William (d. 1779), bookseller, Philadelphia, Pa.

Price's British Carpenter. ¶ *Catalogue* (1760), n.p.

Gaine, Hugh (1726-1807), bookseller, New York, N.Y.
Price's British Carpenter; or, a Treatise on Carpentry. ¶ *Catalogue of books and stationary* (New York: Gaine, 1787), p. 14. EAI: E45073; W116

Hall, David (1714-1772), bookseller, Philadelphia, Pa.
Price's Carpentry. Quarto. ¶ *Catalogue* (1754), broadside. Advertised for sale again in 1761, 1763, 1768, and 1769.

Hall, William (1752-1834), bookseller, Philadelphia, Pa.
Price's Carpentry. Quarto. ¶ *Catalogue* (1774?), broadsheet.

Knox, Henry (1750-1806), bookseller, Boston, Mass.
Price's British Carpenter. Quarto. ¶ *Catalogue* (1773), p. 29.

Lancaster, Pa., Juliana Library Company
Price's British Carpenter; or, A Treatise on Carpentry; containing the most concise and authentic rules of that art; illustrated with sixty-two copperplates. 4th ed. London, 1759. Quarto. ¶ *Catalogue* (1766), p. 37.

Newport, R.I., Redwood Library
Price's British Carpenter. Quarto. ¶ *Catalogue* (1764), p. 7. Identified as the 2d ed., 1735, by Marcus A. McCorison, *The 1764 Catalogue of the Redwood Library Company at Newport, Rhode Island* (New Haven, 1965).

New York, N.Y., Society Library
   Price's (Francis) british carpenter; or a treatise on carpentry. Quarto. ¶ *Catalogue* (1789), p. 56.

Noel, Garrat (fl. 1752-1775), bookseller, New York, N.Y.
   Price's British Carpenter. ¶ *Catalogue* (1759), p. 18.

Noel, Garrat (fl. 1752-75), & Ebenezer Hazard (1744-1817), booksellers, New York, N.Y.
   Price's British Carpenter. ¶ *Catalogue* (1771), p. 18.

Payne, Jonas, & Philip Hearn, booksellers, Savannah, Ga.
   Price's British carpenter, with 62 copper-plates. Octavo. ¶ *Catalogue* (1790), broadside.

Philadelphia, Pa., Library Company
   The British Carpenter; or, A Treatise on Carpentry: Containing the most concise and authentick Rules of that Art: 2d Edition, enlarged. By Francis Price. London, 1735. Quarto. ¶ *Catalogue* (1741), p. 20.

Philadelphia, Pa., Union Library Company
   The British Carpentry: Or a Treatise on Carpentry. Containing the most concise and authentic Rules of that Art, in a more useful and extensive Method than has been before made public. The Third Edition, enlarged and illustrated with 62 Copper Plates. By Francis Price. London, 1753. Quarto. ¶ *Catalogue* (1754), p. 33.

Prichard, William (fl. 1782-1809), bookseller, Philadelphia, Pa.
   Price's British Carpenter, with 62 Copper-plates. Quarto. ¶ *Catalogue* (1785), p. 4.

Rice, Henry (d. 1804), & Company, booksellers, Philadelphia, Pa.
   Price's British Carpenter. ¶ *Catalogue* (1790?), p. 43.

Rice, Henry (d. 1804), & Patrick (fl. 1792-1804), booksellers, Philadelphia, Pa.
   Price's British carpenter. Quarto. ¶ *Catalogue* (1795), p. 60. Advertised for sale again in 1796.

Rivington, James (1724-1802), bookseller, New York, N.Y., & Philadelphia, Pa.
   Price's British Carpenter, or a Concise and easy Treatise on Carpentry, in a more practical Method than has hitherto been made Use of, recommended to the perusal of all Artizans, by the celebrated Hawksmoor, James and Gibbs. ¶ *Catalogue* (1760), p. 46.

Rivington, James (1724-1802), & Samuel Brown (fl. 1755-69), booksellers, New York, N.Y., & Philadelphia, Pa.
   Price's British Carpenter, or a Concise and easy Treatise on Carpentry, in a more practical Method than has hitherto been made Use of, recommended to the perusal of all Artizans, by the celebrated Hawksmoor, James and Gibbs.Folio. ¶ *Catalogue* (1762), p. 68.

Architectural Books in Early America

Sparhawk, John (1730-1803), bookseller, Philadelphia, Pa.
 Price's carpentry. Quarto. ¶ *Catalogue* (1774?), p. 6.

Spotswood, William (1753?-1805), bookseller, Boston, Mass., & Philadelphia, Pa.
 British carpenter; or, a treatise on carpentry. Containing the most concise and authentic rules of that art, in a more useful and extensive method than has been made public. Illustrated with 62 copperplates. By Francis Price. Quarto. ¶ *Catalogue* (1795), p. 52.

Stephens, Thomas (fl. 1793-97), bookseller, Philadelphia, Pa.
 Price's British Carpenter, . . . plates. Quarto. ¶ *A catalogue of books now offered for sale* (Philadelphia: Wrigley & Berriman, 1794), p. 8. Advertised for sale again in 1795. EAI: E27741; W194

110. *Principles of drawing ornaments made easy, by proper examples of leaves for mouldings, capitals, scrolls, husks, foliage, &c. engraved in imitation of drawings, on sixteen plates, with instructions for learning without a master; particularly useful to carvers, cabinet-makers, stucco-workers, painters, smiths, and every one concerned in ornamental decorations. By an artist.* London, 1780. (22.5 x 28cm)

Fenno, John Ward (1778-1802), bookseller, New York, N.Y.
 Principles of drawing Ornaments made easy, 16

plts. ¶ *Catalogue* (1800), p. 5.

111. [Ralph, James (d. 1762)]. *A critical review of the publick buildings, statues and ornaments in, and about London and Westminster. To which is prefix'd, the dimensions of St. Peter's church at Rome, and St. Paul's cathedral at London.* London, 1734. (21cm) Park 68

    Newport, R.I., Redwood Library
    Review of Buildings in and about London. ¶ *Catalogue* (1764), p. 18. Identified as Ralph's *A critical review of the publick buildings, statues and ornaments in, and about London and Westminster*, by McCorison.

112. Rawlins, Thomas. *Familiar architecture; consisting of original designs of houses for gentlemen and tradesmen, parsonages and summer-retreats; with back-fronts, sections, &c. together with banqueting-rooms, churches, and chimney-pieces. To which is added, the masonry of the semicircular and elliptical arches, with practical remarks.* London, 1768. (33cm)

    Fenno, John Ward (1778-1802), bookseller, New York, N.Y.
    Rawlin's Familiar Architecture; or Original Designs of houses for gentlemen and tradesmen, . . . 51 plates. Quarto. ¶ *Catalogue* (1800), p. 4.

113. Richards, Godfrey, tr. *The first book of architecture by Andrea Palladio. Translated out of Italian: with an appendix touching doors and windows, by Pr Le Muet. Translated out of the French, by G.[odfrey] R.[ichards] To which*

are added designs of floors lately made at Somerset-house; and the framing of houses after the best manner of English building, with their proportions and scantlings. London, 1663. (18cm)   Park 69

    Philadelphia, Pa., Loganian Library
        The first book of Architecture, by Andrea Palladio. Translated from the Italian, with an appendix touching doors and windows, by Pr Le Muet, by Godfrey Richards. With plates. London, 1767. Quarto. ¶ *Catalogue* (1795), p. 29.

114. Riou, Stephen (1720-80). *The Grecian orders of architecture. Delineated and explained from the antiquities of Athens, also the parallels of the orders of Palladio, Scamozzi and Vignola, to which are added remarks concerning publick and private edifices with designs.* London, 1768. (48.5cm)   Park 116

    Blake, William Pynson (1769-1820), bookseller, Boston, Mass.
        Riou's Grecian Orders of Architecture. ¶ *Catalogue* (1793), p. 35.

    Guild, Benjamin (1749-92), bookseller, Boston, Mass.
        Rious's Grecian Orders of Architecture. ¶ *Catalogue* (1789), p. 28.

115. Riou, Stephen (1720-80). *Short principles for the architecture of stone-bridges. With practical observations, and a new geometrical diagram to determine the thickness of the piers to the height and base of any given arch.* London, 1760. (22cm)   Park 70

Knox, Henry (1750-1806), bookseller, Boston, Mass.
Riou on the Architecture of Stone Bridges. ¶ *Catalogue* (1773), p. 31.

New York, N.Y., Society Library
Rion [*sic*] on Stone Bridges. Octavo. ¶ *The charter, bye-laws, . . . with a catalogue of the books* (New York: Swords, 1793), p. 71.   EAI: E25915; W179

116. Robinson, William. *Gentleman and builder's director; containing plain and familiar instructions for erecting every kind of building, according to their respective classes, as regulated by an act of Parliament, passed the last sessions.* London, [1774]. (20cm)

Harris, Thaddeus Mason (1768-1842), librarian, Harvard College
Robinson's Gentleman and Builder's Directory. London, 1774. Octavo. ¶ *Selected catalogue of some of the most esteemed publications in the English language. Proper to form a social library: With an introduction upon the choice of books* (Boston: Thomas & Andrews, 1793), p. 19.
EAI: E25587; W173

117. Robinson, William (d.1768). *Proportional architecture; or, the five orders; regulated by equal parts: after so concise a method that renders it useful to all artists and easy to every capacity.* London, 1733. (18cm)

Noel, Garrat (fl. 1752-75), bookseller, New York, N.Y.
Proportional Architecture. ¶ *Catalogue* (1762), p. 27.

118. Rowland, Thomas. *Compleat tables for measuring round and square timber. In two parts.* London, 1745. (narrow octavo)

> Guild, Benjamin (1749-92), bookseller, Boston, Mass.
> Rowland's Timber Measurer. Octavo. ¶ *Catalogue* (1787?), p. 22.

> Hall, David (1714-72), bookseller, Philadelphia, Pa.
> Rowland's complete measurer. Duodecimo. ¶ *Catalogue* (1760?), broadside. Advertised for sale again in 1761 and 1763.

> Rivington, James (1724-1802), & Samuel Brown (fl. 1755-69), booksellers, New York, N.Y., & Philadelphia, Pa.
> Rowland's Tables of Measuring. ¶ *Catalogue* (1762), p. 46.

119. *The rudiments of ancient architecture, in two parts. Containing an historical account of the five orders, with their proportions and examples of each from the antiques; also, Vitruvius on the temples and intercolumniations, &c. of the ancients. Calculated for the use of those who wish to attain a summary knowledge of the science of architecture. With a dictionary of terms. Illustrated with ten plates.* London, 1789. (25cm)

> Fenno, John Ward (1778-1802), bookseller, New York, N.Y.
> Rudiments of Ancient Architecture, containing an historical account of the Five Orders, . . . 11 elegant plates. 2d ed. Octavo. ¶ *Catalogue* (1800), p. 6.

120. *The rudiments of architecture; or, the young workman's instructor. Part first, containing the five orders of columns entire, with frontispieces, doors, windows, porticoes, intercolumniations, and arcades, suited to each; rustick doors and windows; block and cantaliver cornices; rustick quoins; the manner of constructing brick and stone-arches; centuring for groins and vaulting; stairs, twisted rails, roofs and domes; inspectional scales, tables, &c. Directions for drawing plans and elevations with Indian ink: likewise, the French and Spanish orders. Part second; containing geometry; the mensuration of solids and superfices; plain trigonometry, and surveying of land. To which is added, the builder's dictionary. Intended for those whose time will not allow them to attend teachers. Illustrated with upwards of 350 examples, accurately engraved upon thirty-seven large copper-plates.* Edinburgh, 1772. (27cm)

Campbell, Samuel (1763?-1836), bookseller, New York, N.Y.
    The Rudiments of Architecture, or Young Workman's Instructor, with 50 copper-plates. Quarto. ¶ *Catalogue* (1787), p. 27.

121. Rusconi, Giovanni Antonio (ca 1520-1587), tr. *Della architettura di Gio. Antonio Rusconi, con centosessanta figure dissegnate dal medesimo, secondo i precetti di Vitruvio, e con chiarezza, e breuità dichiarte libri dieci.* Venetia, 1590. (30.5cm)   Park 71

Harvard College Library, Cambridge, Mass.
    Rusconi (Giov. Ant.) De l'architettura. Venetia, 1590. Folio. ¶ *Catalogue* (1790), p. 8.

122. Salmon, William (ca. 1703-79). *The builder's guide, and gentleman and trader's assistant; or a universal magazine of tables. Wherein is contained greater variety than in any other book of its kind, with several new and useful tables, never before published; which renders it the most general, complete, and universal companion, for daily use, extant, and highly necessary for all gentlemen, builders, surveyors of buildings, timber measures, carpenters, bricklayers, &c. Also for merchants, shopkeepers, and all tradesmen that deal either by wholesale or retale. Containing tables of timber, board, and plank measure, of square and cubical measure in general, either by the foot, yard or rod. The loads contained in any number of feet, of either rough or squar'd timber, or of plank of any thickness. Of the reduction of brickwork, from 1 foot to 4828 feet, and to any thickness required: what number of bricks are required to build any piece of brickwork, from 1 to 14000 feet, and at any thickness. What number of bricks, lumps, or clinkers laid flat or edge-ways, or of paving tiles or pamants of any size, will pave any floor, of less than 630 foot. What any number of odd feet in a superficial or solid yard comes to, at any price from 1 farthing to 10s. per yard. The value of any number of odd feet of tiling, slating, roofing, flooring, &c. performed by the square of 10 foot squared, at any price from 3s. to 5 or 10s. per square. The value of any number of odd feet of brickwork, or others, performed by the rod square, at any price from 3s. to 10s. per rod. What any number of feet, yards, pounds, ounces, &c. comes to at any price per foot, &c. The value of any odd parts of a hundred at the rate of 112, or 120 to the hundred, at any price from 2s. 6d. to 8s. per hundred. The value of one foot in length of any sort of timber when squared and cut to any scantling fit for building, at any price per foot cubical. A reduction*

of all the common tables of coins, weight and measure. And a perpetual almanack. The whole illustrated by a great variety of examples applicable to the various branches of trade in general, and after so concise a method, that render it useful to all artists, and easy to every capacity. London, 1736. (21cm)   Park 72

Rivington, James (1724-1802), bookseller, New York, N.Y., & Philadelphia, Pa.
    Salmon's Builder's Guide. ¶ *Catalogue* (1760), p. 45.

Rivington, James (1724-1802), & Samuel Brown (fl. 1755-69), booksellers, New York, N.Y., & Philadelphia, Pa.
    Salmon's Builder's Guide. ¶ *Catalogue* (1762), p. 67.

123. Salmon, William, Jr. (ca. 1703-79). *The country builder's estimator: or, the architect's companion. For estimating of new buildings, or repairing of old: in a concise easy method, intirely new; and of use to gentlemen, or their stewards; master-workmen, artificers, or any person that undertakes or letts-out work. Wherein the several artificers works concerned in building, and every article belonging to each of them are fully, distinctly, and separately considered; and the prices thereof inserted, not only of the workmanship, but of the materials also, and what quantity of materials are required to the performance thereof; with the manner of taking dimensions, measuring and valuing the same. To which is added, several new tables, (never before published) for the valuing of oak, or any other timber that is squared and cut to any scantling or size fit*

for building. London, 1737. (16.5cm)   Park 73

Hall, David (1714-74), bookseller, Philadelphia, Pa.
  Salmon's Estimator. ¶*Catalogue* (1763?), broadsheet.

Knox, Henry (1750-1806), bookseller, Boston, Mass.
  Salmon's Builders Estimator. Duodecimo. ¶ *Catalogue* (1773), p. 31.

Rivington, James (1724-1802), bookseller, New York, N.Y., & Philadelphia, Pa.
  Salmon's Builder's Estimater. ¶ *Catalogue* (1760), p. 45.

Rivington, James (1724-1802), & Samuel Brown (fl. 1755-69), booksellers, New York, N.Y., & Philadelphia, Pa.
  Salmon's Builder's Estimator. ¶ *Catalogue* (1762), p. 67.

124. Salmon, William (ca. 1703-79). *The London and country builder's vade mecum: or, the compleat and universal architect's assistant. Comprehending the London and country prices of the different works of bricklayers, masons, carpenters, joyners, glasiers, plumbers, slaters, plaisterers, painters, paviours, carvers, smiths, &c. interspersed with such useful and necessary rules and observations as are of the greatest consequence in estimating of any building. With a great variety of new and useful tables, indispensibly necessary for the more exact and expeditious casting up, or estimating any sort of work.* London, 1745. (20cm)
                                                          Park 74

Beers, Isaac (1742?-1813), bookseller, New Haven, Conn.
Salmon's Builder's Vademecum. ¶ *Catalogue* (1791), p. 23.

Dunlap, William (d. 1779), bookseller, Philadelphia, Pa.
Builder's Vade Mecum. ¶ *Catalogue* (1760), n.p.

Hall, David (1714-74), bookseller, Philadelphia, Pa.
Salmon's Vademecum. ¶ *Catalogue* (1763?), broadsheet.

Noel, Garrat (fl. 1752-75), bookseller, New York, N.Y.
Salmon's Builders Vade Mecum. ¶ *Catalogue* (1755), p. 19.

Rivington, James (1724-1802), bookseller, New York, N.Y., & Philadelphia, Pa.
Salmon's Builder's Vade-mecum. ¶ *Catalogue* (1760), p. 45.

Rivington, James (1724-1802), & Samuel Brown (fl. 1755-69), booksellers, New York, N.Y., & Philadelphia, Pa.
Salmon's Builder's Vade-mecum. ¶ *Catalogue* (1762), p. 67.

Thomas, Isaiah (1749-1831), bookseller, Worcester, Mass., Boston, Mass., & Albany, N.Y.
Salmon's London and Country Builder's Vade Mecum. Octavo. ¶ *Catalogue* (1792), p. 32.

125. Salmon, William (ca. 1703-79). *Palladio Londinensis: or,*

the London art of building. In three parts. Part I. Containing such geometrical problems as are necessary in describing squares, circles, ovals, polygons, arches, and groins. Also the most approved methods for the mensuration of superfices and solids, and these applied to the measuring of all sorts of artificers works, relating to building. Likewise the prices, not of the materials only, but also of the several kinds of works performed by bricklayers, masons, carpenters, joiners, smiths, plaisterers, plumbers, glaziers, painters, pavoirs. . . . Part II. Containing plain and easy directions for the construction of the five orders of architecture, with their pedestals, imposts, arches, elevations, and profiles. The usual mouldings in architecture. Frontispieces, with the several doors proper for each order. Ornaments for doors and windows; all accurately described by modules and minutes. . . . Part III. Contains a description of the several kinds of stair-cases; the various forms of their twisted rails, &c. Also the best rules for framing and trussing all manner of roofs, whether square or bevel. Likewise the ground rules necessary to be observed in architecture and building in general. The whole exemplified on thirty seven copper plates. To which is annexed, the builder's dictionary; containing, an alphabetical explanation of the terms used in architecture. London, 1734. (24cm)   Park 75

Allen, Thomas (fl. 1785-99), bookseller, New York, N.Y.
 London Art of Building. ¶ *Catalogue* (1792), p. 26.

Arnold, Benedict (1741-1801), druggist & bookseller, New Haven, Conn.
 Paladio Londinensis. ¶ *Benedict Arnold, has just*

imported (via New-York) and sells at his store in New-Haven ([New Haven, 1763?]), broadside.
EAI: E41515; W46

Bell, Robert (1731?-84), bookseller, Philadelphia, Pa.
Art of Building, by Palladio, and Salmon. ¶ *Catalogue* (1783), p. 14.

Bradford, William (1719-91), auctioneer, Philadelphia, Pa.
The London Art of Building; the whole illustrated with fifty-four Copper-Plates; to which is annexed the Builder's Dictionary, by William Salmon. ¶ *William Bradford, . . . has imported a collection of books* ([Philadelphia: Bradford, 1760?]), broadside.
EAI: E41433; W35

Hall, David (1714-72), bookseller, Philadelphia, Pa.
London Art of Building. Quarto. ¶ *Catalogue* (1754), broadside. Advertised for sale again in 1763, 1768, and 1769.

Hall, William (1752-1834), bookseller, Philadelphia, Pa.
Salmon's Palladio. Quarto. ¶ *Catalogue* (1774?), broadsheet.

Knox, Henry (1750-1806), bookseller, Boston, Mass.
Salmon's London Art of Building. Quarto. ¶ *Catalogue* (1773), p. 31.

Mein, John (fl. 1760-75), bookseller, Boston, Mass.
Salmon's London Art of building. London, 1762. Quarto. ¶ *Catalogue* (1765), p. 57. Advertised for

sale again in 1766.

Newport, R.I., Redwood Library
Palladio Londinensis. Quarto. ¶ *Catalogue* (1764), p. 7. Identified as the 3d ed., 1748, by McCorison.

Philadelphia, Pa., Library Company
Salmon's (William) London Art of Building. To which is annexed the builder's dictionary. 4th ed. London, 1752. Quarto. ¶ *Catalogue* (1770), n.p.

Providence, R.I., Providence Library
Salmon's Palladio Londinensis. Quarto. ¶ *Catalogue* (1768), p. 15.

Rivington, James (1724-1802), bookseller, New York, N.Y., & Philadelphia, Pa.
Salmon's London new Art of Building. ¶ *Catalogue* (1760), p. 45.

Rivington, James (1724-1802), & Samuel Brown (fl. 1755-69), booksellers, New York, N.Y., & Philadelphia, Pa.
Salmon's London new Art of Building. ¶ *Catalogue* (1762), p. 67.

126. Semple, George (1700?-82?). *A treatise on building in water. In two parts. Part I. Particularly relative to the repair and re-building of Essex-bridge, Dublin, and bridge-building in general, with plans properly suited to the re-building of Ormond-bridge. Part II. Concerning an attempt to contrive and introduce quick and cheap methods, for erecting substantial stone-buildings and other*

works, in fresh and salt water, quaking bogs or morasses, for various purposes; fully laid down and clearly demonstrated, by twelve practical propositions, but not in any case exceeding ten fathom deep: together with a plan for a spacious and a commodious harbour for the downs in England, projecting to 20 feet deep at low water. Principally addressed and peculiarly adapted to young and unexperienced readers. Illustrated with sixty-three copperplates. Dublin, 1776. (28cm)

Baltimore, Md., Library Company
    Building in Water (Art of) by Semple. Quarto. (Given to the library by Mr. George Keatings) ¶ *Catalogue* (1797), p. 7.

Campbell, Samuel (1763?-1836), bookseller, New York, N.Y.
    Temple's [sic] Treatise on Building in Water— illustrated with 63 copper plates. Quarto. ¶ *Catalogue* (1798), p. 24.

New York, N.Y., Society Library
    Semple's building in water. Quarto. ¶ *Catalogue* (1789), p. 64.

Philadelphia, Pa., Library Company
    Semple's treatise on building in water; to which is added, a plan for the general improvement of Ireland—peculiarly adapted for the commercial and landed interest; with plates. London, 1790. ¶ *Catalogue* (1794), p. 9.

Rice, Henry (d. 1804), & Company, booksellers, Phila-

Architectural Books in Early America

delphia, Pa.
>Semple's Art of Building in Water. ¶ *Catalogue* (1790?), p. 43.

Rice, Henry (d. 1804), and Patrick (fl. 1792-1804), booksellers, Philadelphia, Pa.
>Semple's treatise on building in water. Quarto. ¶ *Catalogue* (1795), p. 61. Advertised for sale again in 1796.

127. Serlio, Sebastiano (1475-1554). *Tutte l'opere d'architettura di Sebastiano Serlio Bolognese; doue si trattano in disegno, quelle cose, che sono più necessarie all'architetto, et hora di nuovo aggiunto (oltre il libro delle porte) gran numero di case private nella città, & in villa, et un' indice copiosissimo raccolto per via di considerationi da M. Gio. Domenico Scamozzi.* Venetia, 1584. (25cm)   Park 76

Harvard College Library, Cambridge, Mass.
>Serlio (Sebast.) D'architettura. Venetia, 1584. Quarto. ¶ *Catalogue* (1790), p. 8. Identified by Park as being in the Harvard College Library in 1765.

128. *Several prospects of the most noted publick buildings, in and about the city of London, with a short historical account relating to the same. Plusieurs veues des batiments public les plus considerable tant au dedans qu'a l'entours de la ville de Londres. Avec des remarques historiques sort succinctes, qui les regardent.* London, 1724. (52cm)
>Park 77

Philadelphia, Pa., Library Company

Several Prospects of the most noted public Buildings in and about the City of London; with a short historical Account relating to the same. London, 1724. Quarto. ¶ *The charter, laws, and catalogue of books, of the Library Company of Philadelphia* (Philadelphia: Franklin & Hall, 1764), p. 43.
EAI: E9794; W49

129. Smeaton, John (1724-92). *A narrative of the building and a description of the construction of the Edystone lighthouse with stone: to which is subjoined, an appendix, giving some account of the lighthouse on the Spurn Point, built upon a sand.* London, 1791. (54cm)

   Baltimore, Md., Library Company
   Smeaton's Eddystone Light-House, &c. &c. Folio. ¶ *Catalogue* (1798), p. 48.

   Philadelphia, Pa., Library Company
   Smeaton's narrative of the building, and a description of the construction, of the Edystone Light-house; with an appendix, giving some account of the Light-house on the Spurn Point, built upon sand. With plates. 2d ed. London, 1793. Folio. ¶ *Catalogue* (1794), p. 4.

130. Smith, James. *The carpenters companion: being an accurate and compleat treatise of carpenters works; in which is contained various sorts of timber-floors, partitions, bridges, and especially roofs; with their manner of framing, trussing, &c. made easy to all concerned in building; but more particularly to carpenters; to which is added, the five orders of architecture, in a more easy and concise method*

than any yet published. Exemplified in forty-one copper-plates; with remarks and descriptions. London, 1733. (21cm) Park 78

Mein, John (fl. 1760-75), bookseller, Boston, Mass.
   Carpenter's Companion. ¶ *Catalogue* (1766), p. 22.

Newport, R.I., Redwood Library
   Smith's Carpenter's Companion. Octavo. ¶ *Catalogue* (1764), p. 18.

131. Soane, Sir John (1753-1837). *Designs in architecture; consisting of plans, elevations, and sections, for temples, baths, cassines, pavilions, garden-seats, obelisks, and other buildings; for decorating pleasure-ground, parks, forests, &c. &c. Engraved on 38 copper-plates.* London, 1778. (25.5cm)

   Baltimore, Md., Library Company
      Soane's Designs in Architecture. Folio. ¶ *Catalogue* (1798), p. 8.

   Fenno, John Ward (1778-1802), bookseller, New York, N.Y.
      Soane's Designs, 38 plates. ¶ *Catalogue* (1800), p. 5.

   Philadelphia, Pa., Library Company
      Soane's designs in architecture, consisting of plans, elevations and sections; with plates. London, 1790. Quarto. ¶ *Catalogue* (1794), p. 9.

132. Soane, Sir John (1753-1837). *Plans, elevations, and sections of buildings executed in the counties of Norfolk, Suffolk, Yorkshire, Staffordshire, Warwickshire, Hertfordshire,*

et caetera. London, 1788. (44.5cm)

Philadelphia, Pa., Library Company
Soane's plans, elevations, and sections of buildings; with plates. London, 1793. Folio. ¶ *Catalogue* (1794), p. 4.

Thomas, Isaiah (1749-1831), Ebenezer Turrell Andrews (1766-1851), & Obadiah Penniman (1776-1820), booksellers, Albany, N.Y.
Plans, Elevations and Situations of Buildings, &c. by John Soane. ¶ *Catalogue* (1797?), p. 33.

133. Sousa Coutinho, Manuel de, called Luis de Sousa (1555?-1632). *Plans, elevations, sections, and views of the church of Batalha in the province of Estremadura in Portugal, with the history and description . . . with remarks, to which is prefixed an introductory discourse on the principles of Gothic architecture by James Murphy* [1760-1814]. London, 1795. (54cm)

Baltimore, Md., Library Company
Murphy's Plans, &c. of the Church of Batalha. Folio. ¶ *Catalogue* (1798), p. 48.

134. Swan, Abraham. *The British architect: or, the builder's treasury of stair-cases. Containing, I. An easier, more intelligible, and expeditious method of drawing the five orders, than has hitherto been published, by a scale of twelve equal parts, free from those troublesome divisions call'd aliquot parts. Shewing also how to glue up their columns and capitals. II. Likewise stair-cases, (those most useful, ornamental, and necessary parts of a building, though*

never before sufficiently described in any book, ancient or modern); shewing their most convenient situation, and the form of their ascending in the most grand manner: with a great variety of curious ornaments, whereby any gentleman may fix on what will suit him best, there being examples of all kinds; and necessary directions for such persons as are unacquainted with that branch. III. Designs of arches, doors, and windows. IV. A great variety of new and curious chimney-pieces, in the most elegant and modern taste. V. Corbels, shields, and other beautiful decorations. VI. Several useful and necessary rules of carpentry; with the manner of truss'd roofs, and the nature of a splay'd circular soffit, both in a streight and circular wall, never published before. Together with raking cornices, groins, and angle brackets, described. The whole being illustrated with upwards of one hundred designs and examples, curiously engraved by the best hands, on sixty folio copper-plates. London, 1745. First American edition 1775. (39.5cm)

Park 79, Hitchcock 1248-49

Bell, Robert (1731?-84), bookseller, Philadelphia, Pa.
    British Architect, containing above 100 designs and Examples, by Abraham Swan, Architect. ¶ *Catalogue* (1783), p. 21.

Blake, William Pynson (1769-1820), bookseller, Boston, Mass.
    Swan's British Architect. ¶ *Catalogue* (1793), p. 38. Advertised for sale again in 1796.

Blake, William Pynson (1769-1820), & Lemuel (1775-1861), booksellers, Boston, Mass.
    Swan's British Architect. ¶ *Catalogue* (1798), p. 40.

Campbell, Robert (d. 1800), bookseller, Philadelphia, Pa.
>   Swan's British architect, or the builder's treasury of stair-cases. ¶ *Catalogue* (1794), p. 54. Advertised for sale again in 1796 and 1797.

Campbell, Samuel (1763?-1836), bookseller, New York, N.Y.
>   Swan's British Architect: or the Builder's Treasury of Staircases—engraved on 60 copper plates. Folio. ¶ *Catalogue* (1798), p. 23.

Cox, Edward (fl. 1766-78), & Edward Berry (fl. 1766-72), booksellers, Boston, Mass.
>   Swan's British Architecture. Folio. ¶ *Catalogue* (1772?), p. 26.

Gaine, Hugh (1726-1807), bookseller, New York, N.Y.
>   Swan's British Architect; or, the Builder's Treasury. ¶ *Catalogue* (1787), p. 16.

Hall, David (1714-72), bookseller, Philadelphia, Pa.
>   Swan's British Architect Folio. ¶ *Catalogue* (1754), broadside. Advertised for sale again in 1761, 1767, 1768, and 1769.

New York, N.Y., Society Library
>   Swan's (Abraham) british architect, or the builder's treasury, with one hundred designs and examples, curiously engraved on sixty copperplates. Folio. ¶ *Catalogue* (1792), p. 124.

Noel, Garrat (fl. 1752-75), & Ebenezer Hazard (1744-

1817), booksellers, New York, N.Y.
    Swan's British Architecture, or Builder's Treasury. ¶ *Catalogue* (1771), p. 18.

Philadelphia, Pa., Library Company
    Swan (Abraham) his British Architect; or, the Builder's Treasury of Stair-Cases. Illustrated with upwards of one hundred Designs and Examples, curiously Engraved by the best hands, on sixty Folio Copperplates. London. Folio. ¶ *Catalogue* (1775), p. 55.

Rice, Henry (d. 1804), & Patrick (fl. 1792-1804), booksellers, Philadelphia, Pa.
    Swan's British architect or builders treasury. ¶ *Catalogue* (1795), p. 61. Advertised for sale again in 1796.

Sparhawk, John (1730-1803), bookseller, Philadelphia, Pa.
    Swan's British architecture. Folio. ¶ *Catalogue* (1774?), p. 2.

Spotswood, William (1753?-1805), bookseller, Boston, Mass., & Philadelphia, Pa.
    British architect; or, the builder's treasury of staircases. Illustrated with upwards of 100 designs and examples, curiously engraved on 60 folio copper plates. By Abraham Swan, architect. Folio. ¶ *Catalogue* (1795), p. 52.

Thomas, Isaiah (1749-1831), Ebenezer Turrell Andrews (1766-1851), & Obadiah Penniman (1776-1820), book-

sellers, Albany, N.Y.
British Architect, or Builders' Treasury, by Abraham Swan. ¶ *Catalogue* (1797?), p. 33.

Young, William (1755-1829), bookseller, Philadelphia, Pa.
Swan's Builder's Treasury. Folio. ¶ *Catalogue* (1786), p. 24.

135. Swan, Abraham. *A collection of designs in architecture, containing new plans and elevations of houses, for general use. With a great variety of sections of rooms; from a common room, to the most grand and magnificent. Their decorations, viz. bases, surbases, architraves, freezes, and cornices, properly inriched with foliages, frets and flowers, in a new and grand taste. With margins and mouldings for the panelling. All large enough for practice. To which are added, curious designs of stone and timber bridges, extending from twenty feet to two hundred and twenty, in one arch. Likewise some screens and pavilions. In two volumes. Each containing sixty plates, curiously engraved on copper.* London, 1757. First American edition 1775. (42.5cm) Park 80, Hitchcock 1250

Beers, Isaac (1742?-1813), bookseller, New Haven, Conn.
Swan's Architecture. ¶ *Catalogue* (1791), p. 23.

Bradford, Thomas (1745-1838), bookseller, Philadelphia, Pa.
Swan's architecture. ¶ *Catalogue* (1796), p. 56.

Cox, Edward (fl. 1766-78), & Edward Berry (fl.

1766-72), booksellers, Boston, Mass.
    Swan's Designs. 2 vols. Folio. ¶ *Catalogue* (1772?), p. 26.

Guild, Benjamin (1749-92), bookseller, Boston, Mass.
    Swan's Designs, in Architecture. ¶ *Catalogue* (1789), p. 31.

Hall, David (1714-72), bookseller, Philadelphia, Pa.
    Swan's designs, and architecture. ¶ *Catalogue* (1763?), broadsheet. Advertised for sale again in 1767, 1768, and 1769

Hall, William (1752-1834), bookseller, Philadelphia, Pa.
    Swan's Designs. Folio. ¶ *Catalogue* (1774?), broadsheet.

Larkin, Ebenezer (1767-1813), bookseller, Boston, Mass.
    Architecture, Swan's. ¶ *Catalogue* (1798), p. 6.

Noel, Garrat (fl. 1752-75), bookseller, New York, N.Y.
    Swan's Architecture. ¶ *Catalogue* (1762), p. 27.

Noel, Garrat (fl. 1752-75), & Ebenezer Hazard (1744-1817), booksellers, New York, N.Y.
    Swan's Collection of Designs in Architecture. ¶ *Catalogue* (1771), p. 18.

Philadelphia, Pa., Association Library Company
    Architecture, design of, by Swan. 2 vols. London, 1757. Folio. ¶ *Catalogue* (1765), p. [21].

Philadelphia, Pa., Library Company

Architecture; (A Collection of Designs in) containing new plans and elevations of houses, for general use; with a great variety of sections of rooms, and their decorations in a new and grand taste. To which are added, curious designs of stone and timber bridges, extending from 20 feet to 220 feet, in one arch; likewise some screens and pavilions. By Abraham Swan, Architect. 2 vols. London, 1757. Folio. ¶ *Catalogue* (1770), n.p.

Swan's (Abraham) Collection of Designs in Architecture, containing new plans and elevations of houses for general use. With a great variety of sections of rooms, from a common room to the most grand and magnificent; with their decorations. To which are added, curious designs of stone and timber bridges, &c. 2 vols. London, 1767. Folio. (Given to the library by David Evans) ¶ *Catalogue* (1770), n.p.

Philadelphia, Pa., Union Library Company
Architecture (Designs on) by Swan. Folio. ¶ *Catalogue* (1765), p. 1.

Rivington, James (1724-1802), bookseller, New York, N.Y., & Philadelphia, Pa.
Swann's Architecture. ¶ *Catalogue* (1760), p. 45.

Rivington, James (1724-1802), & Samuel Brown (fl. 1755-69), booksellers, New York, N.Y., & Philadelphia, Pa.
Swann's Architecture. ¶ *Catalogue* (1762), p. 67.

Sparhawk, John (1730-1803), bookseller, Philadelphia, Pa.
> Swan's designs. Folio. ¶ *Catalogue* (1774?), p. 2.

Young, William (1755-1829), bookseller, Philadelphia, Pa.
> Swan's Collection of Designs in Architecture, exhibiting new plans and Elevations of Houses, &c. 2 vols. ¶ *Catalogue* (1786), p. 24.

136. Swan, Abraham. *Designs in carpentry, containing domes, trussed roofs, flooring, trussing of beams, angle-brackets, and cornices.* London, 1759. (27cm)   Park 81

Later edition published under the title: *The carpenter's complete instructor, in several hundred designs, consisting of domes, trussed roofs, and various cupolas: with the methods of securing them on the roofs, for churches, chapels, houses, and other buildings. Shewing the most approved manner of lighting stair-cases, with various sorts of lanthorns, in a new and elegant taste, explaining the manner of piecing beams, or plating, or any sort of bandage, for timber spires for churches, &c. truss partitions, framing of flooring, trussing of beams, angle brackets, cornices, coving, forms of groins, hips, &c. To which is annexed, a great variety of timber bridges, of various dimensions.* London, 1768. (26.5cm)   Park 81

Bell, Robert (1731?-84), bookseller, Philadelphia, Pa.
> Swan's Designs in Carpentry, on 50 Plates. Quarto. ¶ *Catalogue* (1773), p. [48].

Carpenter's Complete Instructor, in several hundred Designs by Abraham Swan, Architect. ¶ *Catalogue* (1783), p. 27.

Blake, William Pynson (1769-1820), & Lemuel (1775-1861), booksellers, Boston, Mass.
    Swan's Carpenter's Complete Instructor. ¶ *Catalogue* (1798), p. 40.

Bradford, Thomas (1745-1838), bookseller, Philadelphia, Pa.
    Swan's carpenter's instructor. Folio. ¶ *Catalogue* (1796), p. 56.

Campbell, Samuel (1763?-1836), bookseller, New York, N.Y.
    Swan's Carpenters Complete Instructor, with 55 plates. Quarto. ¶ *Catalogue* (1787), p. 17.

Noel, Garrat (fl. 1752-75), & Ebenezer Hazard (1744-1817), booksellers, New York, N.Y.
    Swan's Carpenter's complete Instructor in several Hundred Designs for Churches, Chapels, Houses, Timber Bridges, and other Buildings. ¶ *Catalogue* (1771), p. 36.

Sparhawk, John (1730-1803), bookseller, Philadelphia, Pa.
    Swan's carpentry. Quarto. ¶ *Catalogue* (1774?), p. 6.

137. Swan, Abraham. *Designs for chimnies, and the proportions they bear to their respective rooms containing more than eighty examples of that kind. Also variety of arches,*

doors and windows; to which is added a concise but clear description of the five orders, regulated by a scale of twelve equal parts. With some observations on rules and methods used in drawing. The whole neatly engraved on fifty octavo copper-plates. London, [1765]. (21.5cm)

Later edition published under the title: *Upwards of one hundred and fifty new designs, for chimney pieces; from the plain and simple, to the most superb and magnificent, properly adapted to rooms, halls, saloons, lobbies, &c. of every dimension; with the proportions they bear to each, and full and complete instructions to workmen; enriched with a great variety of arches, doors, windows, cornices, architraves, ornaments for trusses, pedestals, pediments, columns, imposts, modillions, soffets, &c. To which is added, a concise and clear description of the five orders of architecture, regulated by a scale of twelve equal parts; with observations on rules and methods to be observed in drawing the whole. By Abraham Swan, architect. Adorned with fifty-four copper-plates, elegantly engraved.* London, 1768. (23cm)   Park 82

Knox, Henry (1750-1806), bookseller, Boston, Mass.
   Swan's Designs for Chimneys. Octavo. ¶ *Catalogue* (1773), p. 32.

138. Vardy, John (d. 1765). *Some designs of Mr. Inigo Jones and Mr. Wm. Kent.* [London], 1744. (42.5cm)

Bradford, Thomas (1745-1838), bookseller, Philadelphia, Pa.
   Varley's designs. Folio. ¶ *Catalogue* (1796), p. 56. Identified as Vardy's *Some designs of Mr. Inigo Jones*

and Mr. Wm. Kent, by Johnston.

139. Vignola, Giacomo Barozzi, da (1507-73). *Regola delli cinque ordini d'architettura di M. Iacomo Barozzio da Vignola.* [Roma, 1563?]. (37cm)　　　　Park 2

　Reigle des cinq ordres d'architecture. Paris, 1653. (39cm)

　Clarkson, Matthew (1758-1825), & Ebenezer Hazard (1744-1817), estate administrators, Philadelphia, Pa.
　　　Architecture, viz. De Vignole. . . . Cuts. Quarto.
　　　¶ *Catalogue* (1785), broadside.

　Harvard College Library, Cambridge, Mass.
　　　Barozzio (Jacomo) Regola delli cinque ordini d'architettura, Stampa in Roma, 1617. Folio. ¶ *Catalogue* (1790), p. 8. Identified by Park as being in the Harvard College Library in 1765.

140. Vitruvius Pollio. *De architectura [libri decem].* Roma, ca. 1483-90. (28cm)　　　　Park 83

　Harvard College Library, Cambridge, Mass.
　　　Vitruvius (Luc. Pollio) Di architecturi. Como, 1521. Folio. ¶ *Catalogue* (1790), p. 8. Identified by Park as being in the Harvard College Library in 1765.

　　　Vitruvius (Luc. Pollio) Dell'architecttura. Venetia, 1584. Quarto. ¶ *Catalogue* (1790), p. 8. Identified by Park as being in the Harvard College Library in 1765.

Philadelphia, Pa., Loganian Library
  Vitruvii Pollionis de Architectura libri cum not. variorum. Henr. Wotton elementa Architecturae. Bernhardini Baldi lexicon Vitruvianum, et explicatio scamillorum imparium Vitruvii. Leo. Bapt. de Albertis libri de Pictura. Excerpta e dialogo Pomponii Gauvici de Sculptura & Lud. Demontiosii de Sculptura &c. Pictura commentariis; Omnia in unum collecta a Joh. de Lact. Amsterdam, 1649. Folio. ¶ *Catalogue* (1760), p. 101.

141. Wallis, N. *The complete modern joiner, or a collection of original designs in the present taste, for chimney-pieces and door-cases, with their mouldings and enrichments at large; frizes, tablets, ornaments for pilasters, bases, sub-bases and cornices for rooms, &c. with a table shewing the proportion of chimneys and their entablatures, to rooms of any size: by N. Wallis, architect. A new edition.—Neatly engraved on thirty-six plates.* 2d ed. London, [1772]. (21.5 x 28cm)

White, James (1755?-1824), bookseller, Boston, Mass.
  Carpenters complete modern Joiner, or the present taste of chimney pieces & door cases. ¶ *Catalogue* (1797?), p. 8.

142. Ware, Isaac (d. 1766). *A complete body of architecture. Adorned with plans and elevations, from original designs. By Isaac Ware, esq. of his majesty's board of works. In which are interspersed some designs of Inigo Jones, never before published.* 2 vols. London, 1756. (42.5cm) Park 84

Martin, William, bookseller, Boston, Mass.
  Architecture by Ware. ¶ *Catalogue of Martin's*

Circulating Library ([Boston]: Freeman, 1786), p. [3]. EAI: E44915; W111

Philadelphia, Pa., Library Company
A Compleat Body of Architecture, adorned with Plans and Elevations from original Designs. By Isaac Ware, Esq; In which are dispersed some Designs of Inigo Jones, never before published. 1756. Folio. ¶ *The charter, laws, and catalogue of books, of the Library Company of Philadelphia* (Philadelphia: Franklin & Hall, 1764), p. 26.
EAI: E9794; W49

143. Ware, Isaac (d. 1766). *Designs of Inigo Jones and others published by I: Ware.* [London, ca. 1735]. (23.5cm)
Park 85

Hall, David (1714-72), bookseller, Philadelphia, Pa.
Designs of Inigo Jones and others. Quarto. ¶ *Catalogue* (1754), broadside. Advertised for sale again in 1761.

144. Ware, Isaac (d. 1766), tr. *The four books of Andrea Palladio's architecture: wherein, after a short treatise of the five orders, those observations that are most necessary in building, private houses, streets, bridges, piazzas, xisti, and temples are treated of.* 4 vols. in 1. London, 1738. (40cm)
Park 86

Bell, Robert (1731?-84), bookseller, Philadelphia, Pa.
Palladio's Architecture, on 99 plates, by Ware. ¶ *Catalogue* (1783), p. 62.

Guild, Benjamin (1749-92), bookseller, Boston, Mass.
Palladio's Architecture. 1 vol. ¶ *Catalogue* (1789), p. 25.

Hall, David (1714-72), bookseller, Philadelphia, Pa.
Ware's palladio Londinensis. ¶ *Catalogue* (1763?), broadsheet. Advertised for sale again in 1767, 1768, and in 1769 as Palladio's *Four books of architecture* (Folio).

Hall, William (1752-1834), bookseller, Philadelphia, Pa.
Ware's Palladio. Folio. ¶ *Catalogue* (1774?), broadsheet.

Newport, R.I., Redwood Library
Ware's Palladio. Folio. ¶ *Catalogue* (1764), p. 6.

New York, N.Y., Society Library
Palladio's (Andrea) architecture, in four books, containing, 1st, the five orders, and the most necessary observations in building—2d, in which the designs of several houses ordered by him, both within and out the city, are comprised, and the designs of the ancient houses of the greeks and latins—3d, wherein the ways, bridges, piazzas, basilicas, and xisti, are treated of—4th, describing and figuring the ancient temples that are in Rome, and some others that are in Italy and out of Italy, literally translated from the original latin by Isaac Ware, esquire. Folio. ¶ *Catalogue* (1791), p. 98.

Philadelphia, Pa., Library Company

Palladio's (Andrea) Architecture: wherein, after a short treatise of the five orders, those observations, that are most necessary in building private houses, streets, bridges, piazzas, and temples are treated of. By Isaac Ware. London, 1738. Folio. ¶ *Catalogue* (1770), n.p.

Philadelphia, Pa., Union Library Company
The Four Books of Andrea Polladio's Architecture: Wherein after a short Treatise of the Five Orders, those Observations that are most necessary in Building private Houses, Streets, Bridges, Piazzas, Xisti, and Temples, are treated of. London, published by Isaac Ware, 1738. Folio. ¶ *Catalogue* (1754), p. 31.

Rivington, James (1724-1802), bookseller, New York, N.Y., & Philadelphia, Pa.
Ware's Palladios System of Architecture. ¶ *Catalogue* (1760), p. 45.

Rivington, James (1724-1802), & Samuel Brown (fl. 1755-69), booksellers, New York, N.Y., & Philadelphia, Pa.
Ware's Palladio's System of Architecture. ¶ *Catalogue* (1762), p. 67.

145. Wood, John (1728-81). *A series of plans for cottage or habitations of the labourer, either in husbandry, or the mechanic arts, adapted as well to towns, as to the country. Engraved on thirty plates. To which is added, an introduction, containing many useful observations on this class of building; tending to the comfort of the poor and*

advantage of the builder: with calcultions of expences. By the late Mr. J. Wood, of Bath, architect. A new edition. London, 1792. First edition 1781? (36cm)

Fenno, John Ward (1778-1802), bookseller, New York, N.Y.
    Wood's Cottages, . . . 30 plates. Quarto. ¶ *Catalogue* (1800), p. 4.

146. Wren, Sir Christopher (1675-1747). *Parentalia: or, memoirs of the family of the Wrens; viz. of Mathew bishop of Ely, Christopher dean of Windsor, &c. but chiefly of Sir Christopher Wren, late surveyor-general of the royal buildings, president of the royal society, &c. &c. In which is contained, besides his works, a great number of original papers and records; on religion, politicks, anatomy, mathematicks, architecture, antiquities; and most branches of polite literature. Compiled by his son Christopher; now published by his grandson, Stephen Wren, esq; with the care of Joseph Ames, F.R.S. and secretary to the Society of Antiquaries, London.* London, 1750. (35.5cm)

    Charleston, S.C., Library Society
        Wren's parentalia, or memoirs of the family of the Wrens. London, 1750. Folio. ¶ *Catalogue* (1770), p. 10.

147. Wrighte, William. *Grotesque architecture, or, rural amusement; consisting of plans, elevations, and sections, for huts, retreats, summer and winter hermitages, terminaries, Chinese, Gothic, and natural grottos, cascades, baths, mosques, moresque pavilions, grotesque and rustic seats, green houses, &c. Many of which may be executed with*

flints, irregular stones, rude branches, and roots of trees. The whole containing twenty-eight entire new designs, beautifully engraved on copper plates, with scales to each. To which is added, a full explanation, in letter press, and the true method of executing them. London, 1767. (22.5cm)

Fenno, John Ward (1778-1802), bookseller, New York, N.Y.

> Grotesque Architecture, or plans, elevations, and sections for Huts, Hermitages, Terminaries, Chinese, Gothic, and Natural Grottos, Cascades, Baths, Mosques, Moresque Pavilions, Green-houses, &c. containing 28 new designs. ¶ *Catalogue* (1800), pp. 5-6.

APPENDIX A

Publication Dates and Imprints of Books Cited,
in Order of Number of References

	Number of Booksellers/ Libraies	Earliest Publication Date	Earliest American Catalogue Reference	# in Helen Park's *List*
109. Price, *The British carpenter*	27	1733 London	1741	HP67
59. Langley, *The builder's jewel*	25	1741 London	1760	HP41
98. Pain, *The practical builder*	20	1774 London	1792	—
47. Hoppus, *Practical measuring*	19	1736 London	1760	HP32
44. Hawney, *The compleat measurer*	18	1717 London	1762	HP106
94. Pain, *The builder's pocket-treasure*	16	1763 London	1773	HP64
134. Swan, *The British architect*	16	1745 London	1754	HP79
135. Swan, *A collection of designs in architecture*	16	1757 London	1760	HP80
87. [Norman], *The town and country builder's assistant*	15	1786 Boston	1787	—

163

125.	Salmon, *Palladio Londinensis*	13	1734 London	1754	HP75
5.	*The builder's dictionary*	11	1734 London	1741	HP4
57.	Langley, *The builder's compleat assistant*	10	1738 London	1761?	HP39
96.	Pain, *The carpenter's pocket directory*	10	1781 London	1787	—
97.	Pain, *Pain's British Palladio*	10	1786 London	1793	—
99.	Pain, *The practical house carpenter*	10	2d ed. 1788 London	1796	—
144.	Ware, *The four books of Andrea Palladio's architecture*	10	1738 London	1754	HP86
93.	Pain, *The builder's companion*	9	1758 London	1760	HP63
29.	Gibbs, *A book of architecture*	8	1728 London	1760	HP17
37.	Halfpenny, *A new and compleat systen of architecture*	8	1749 London	1762	HP23
43.	Halfpenny, *Useful architecture*	8	1752 London	1757	HP30

58.	Langley, *The builder's director*	8	1747 London	1762	HP40
60.	Langley, *The city and country builder's, and workman's treasury of designs*	8	1740 London	1754	HP42
30.	Gibbs, *Rules for drawing the several parts of architecture*	7	1732 London	1754	HP18
67.	Leoni, *The architecture of A. Palladio*	7	1715-19 London	1741	HP47
124.	Salmon, *The London and country builder's vade mecum*	7	1745 London	1755	HP74
16.	Crunden, *Convenient and ornamental architecture*	6	1767 London	1773	HP10
36.	Halfpenny, *The modern builder's assistant*	6	1742 London	1759	HP22
46.	Hoppus, *The gentleman's and builder's repository*	6	1737 London	1754	HP31
126.	Semple, *A treatise on building in water*	6	1776 Dublin	1789	—
136.	Swan, *Designs in carpentry; The carpenter's complete instructor*	6	1759 London	1771	HP81

28.	Gauger, *La mechanique du feu; Fires improved*	5	1713 Paris; 1715 London	1741	—
64.	Langley, *The workman's golden rule*	5	1750 London	1760	HP45
78.	Morris, *Architecture improved*	5	1755 London	1760	HP52
83.	[Neve], *The city and countrey purchaser*	5	1703 London	1743	HP58
92.	Over, *Ornamental architecture*	5	1758 London	1760	HP61
13.	Columbani, *A new book of ornaments*	4	1775 London	1796	—
17.	Crunden, *The joyner and cabinet-maker's darling*	4	1765 London	1793	HP11
26.	Fréart, *Parallele de l'architecture antique et de la moderne; A parallel of the ancient architecture with the modern*	4	1650 Paris; 1664 London	1693	HP15
27.	Garret, *Designs and estimates, of farm houses*	4	1747 London	1762	HP16
51.	Jores, *A new book of iron work*	4	1759 London	1762	HP34
56.	Langley, *The builder's chest-book*	4	1727 London	1760	HP38

Architectural Books in Early America

70.	Lightoler, *The gentleman and farmer's architect*	4	1762 London	1766	HP50
95.	Pain, *The carpenter's and joiner's repository*	4	1778 London	1787?	—
123.	Salmon, *The country builder's estimator*	4	1737 London	1760	HP73
4.	Benjamin, *The country builder's assistant*	3	1797 Greenfield Mass.	1799	—
7.	Campbell, *Vitruvius Britannicus*	3	1715-71 London	1741	HP5
21.	*Designs for chimney-pieces*	3	1793 London	1797?	—
35.	Halfpenny, *The country gentleman's pocket companion*	3	1753 London	1760	HP21
38.	Halfpenny, *Practical architecture*	3	1724? London	1760	HP26
45.	Hodgson, *The complete measurer*	3	7th ed. 1779 Dublin	1790	—
49.	Jones (I.), *The most notable antiquity of Great Britain*	3	1655 London	1693	—
52.	Keay, *The practical measurer*	3	1718 London	1755	HP35

55.	Langley, *Ancient masonry*	3	1736 London	1765	HP37
66.	Le Clerc, *Traité d'architecture; A treatise of architecture*	3	1714 Paris; 1723-24 London	1759	HP46
80.	Morris, *Select architecture*	3	1755 London	1760	HP55
86.	Nicholson, *The student's instructor in drawing and working the five orders of architecture*	3	1795 London	1797?	—
102.	Peacock, *Οἰκίδια, or, nutshells*	3	1785 London	1789	—
105.	Perrault (Claude), *Ordonnance des cinq especes de colones; A treatise of the five orders of columns in architecture*	3	1683 Paris; 1708 London	1723	HP66
118.	Rowland, *Compleat tables for measuring round and square timber*	3	1745 London	1760?	—
131.	Soane, *Designs in architecture*	3	1778 London	1790	—
1.	Adam, *The works in architecture*	2	1773-1822 London	1775	HP1

3.	Anderson, *A practical treatise on chimneys*	2	1776 Edinburgh	1789	—
6.	*The builder's price-book*	2	1785 London	1793	—
11.	Chambers, *A treatise on civil architecture*	2	1759 London	1790	HP7
12.	Coggeshall, *The art of measuring*	2	5th ed. 1732 London	1760	—
14.	Columbani, *Variety of capitals, freezes, and corniches*	2	1776 London	1796	—
23.	Espie, *Maniere de rendre toutes sortes d'édifices incombustibles; The manner of securing all sorts of buildings from fire*	2	1754 Paris; 1755 London	1768?	—
40.	Halfpenny, *Rural architecture in the Gothic taste*	2	1752 London	1760	HP27
41.	Halfpenny, *Twelve beautiful designs for farm-houses*	2	1750 London	1762	HP28
48.	Hutton, *Principles of bridges*	2	1772 Newcastle	1791	—
53.	Kent, *The designs of Inigo Jones*	2	1727 London	1793	HP36

62.	Langley, *The London prices of bricklayer materials and works*	2	1748 London	1772?	HP109
68.	Leoni, *The architecture of Leon Battista Alberti*	2	1726 London	1765	HP48
69.	Leybourn, *The mirror of architecture*	2	1669 London	1758	HP49
71.	Lock & Copland, *A new book of ornaments*	2	1752 London	1771	HP8
72.	Mandey, *Mellificum mensionis*	2	1682 London	1734	HP111
75.	Middleton, *Picturesque and architectural views*	2	1793 London	1797	—
76.	Miller, *Andrea Palladio's Elements of architecture*	2	ca.1748 London	1771	HP51
79.	Morris, *Lectures on architecture*	2	1734-36 London	1773	HP53
81.	Morrison, *Useful and ornamental designs in architecture*	2	1793 Dublin?	1795	—
85.	Nicholson, *The carpenter's new guide*	2	1793 London	1797?	—
108.	Pool, *Views of the most remarkable public buildings, monuments and other edifices in the city of Dublin*	2	1780 Dublin	1794	—

114.	Riou, *The Grecian orders of architecture*	2	1768 London	1789	HP116
115.	Riou, *Short principles for the architecture of stone-bridges*	2	1760 London	1773	HP70
122.	Salmon, *The builder's guide*	2	1736 London	1760	HP72
129.	Smeaton, *Narrative of the building... of the Edystone lighthouse*	2	1791 London	1794	—
130.	Smith, *The carpenter's companion*	2	1733 London	1764	HP78
132.	Soane, *Plan, elevations, and sections of buildings*	2	1788 London	1794	—
139.	Vignola, *Regola delli cinque ordini d'architettura*	2	1563 Rome or Venice	1785	HP2
140.	Vitruvius, *De architectura*	2	1483-90 Rome	1760	HP83
142.	Ware, *A complete body of architecture*	2	1756 London	1764	HP84
2.	Alberti, *L'architettura*	1	1550 Florence	1723	—
8.	*The carpenters rules of work in the town of Boston*	1	1774 Boston	1798	—

9.	Castell, *The villas of the ancients*	1	1728 London	1757	HP6
10.	Chambers, *Designs of Chinese buildings*	1	1757 London	1770	—
15.	[Crunden], *The carpenter's companion for Chinese railing and gates*	1	1765 London	1797?	HP9
18.	Darly, *A compleat body of architecture*	1	1773 London	1796	—
19.	Decker, *Chinese architecture*	1	1759 London	1760	HP12
20.	Desgodets, *Les édifices antiques de Rome; The ancient buildings of Rome*	1	1682 Paris; 1795 London	1798	—
22.	*Designs for shop-fronts and door-cases*	1	179-? London	1797?	—
24.	Félebién, *Des principes de l'architecture*	1	1676 Paris	1785	—
25.	Ferrerio, *Palazzi di Roma*	1	1655 Rome	1785	HP14
31.	Good, *Measuring made easy*	1	1719 London	1794	—
32.	Halfpenny, *The art of sound building*	1	1725 London	1796	HP19

33.	[Halfpenny], *The builder's pocket companion*	1	1728 London	1767	HP20
34.	Halfpenny, *Chinese and Gothic architecture*	1	1752 London	1762	—
39.	Halfpenny, *Rural architecture in the Chinese taste*	1	2d ed. 1752 London	1796	—
42.	Halfpenny, *Twenty new designs of Chinese lattice*	1	1750 London	1760	HP29
50.	Jones (W.), *The gentlemens or builders companion*	1	ca.1735? London?	1773	—
54.	Laing, *Hints for dwellings*	1	1800 London	1800	—
61.	Langley, *Gothic architecture*	1	1747 London	1771	HP43
63.	Langley, *Practical geometry*	1	1726 London	1746	HP44
65	Laugier, *Essai sur l'architecture; An essay on architecture*	1	1753 Paris; 1755 London	1783	—
73.	Manwaring, *The carpenter's compleat guide*	1	1765 London	1797?	—
74.	[Middleton], *Decorations for parks and gardens*	1	1800? London	1800	—

Architectural Books in Early America

77.	Miller, *The country gentleman's architect*	1	1787 London	1800	—
82.	Moxon, *The theory and practice of architecture; or, Vitruvius and Vignola abridged*	1	5th ed. 1702-03 London	1760	HP57
84.	Nicholson, *The carpenter and joiner's assistant*	1	1792? London	1800	—
88.	Oakley, *Every man a compleat builder*	1	1738 London	1796	HP59
89.	Oakley, *The magazine of architecture*	1	1730 Westminster	1764	HP60
90.	*Ornamental iron work*	1	1800? London	1800	—
91.	*Ornaments displayed*	1	178-? London	1800	—
100.	Paine, *Plans, elevations and sections of noblemen and gentlemen's houses*	1	1767-83 London	1797	—
101.	Palladio, *I quattro libri dell'architettura*	1	1570 Venice	1790	HP65
103.	Perrault (Charles), *Parallele des anciens et des modernes*	1	1688-97 Paris	1795	—
104.	Perrault (Claude), *Architecture générale de Vitruve*	1	1681 Amsterdam	1783	—

174

106. Plaw, *Ferme ornée*	1	1795 London	1798	—
107. Plaw, *Sketches for country houses*	1	1800 London	1800	—
110. *The principles of drawing ornaments made easy*	1	1780 London	1800	—
111. Ralph, *A critical review of the publick buildings, statues and ornaments in, and about London and Westminster*	1	1734 London	1764	HP68
112. Rawlins, *Familiar architecture*	1	1768 London	1800	—
113. Richards, *The first book of architecture, by Andrea Palladio*	1	1663 London	1795	HP69
116. Robinson, *Gentleman and builder's director*	1	1774 London	1793	—
117. Robinson, *Proportional architecture*	1	1733 London	1762	—
119. *The rudiments of ancient architecture*	1	1789 London	1800	—
120. *The rudiments of architecture*	1	1772 Edinburgh	1787	—
121. Rusconi, *Della architettura*	1	1590 Venice	1790	HP71

Architectural Books in Early America

127. Serlio, *Tutte l'opere d'architettura*	1	1584 Venice	1790	HP76
128. *Several prospects of the most noted publick buildings, in and about the city of London*	1	1724 London	1764	HP77
133. Sousa Coutinho, *Plans, elevations, sections and views of the church of Batalha*	1	1795 London	1798	—
137. Swan, *Designs for chimnies*	1	1765 London	1773	HP82
138. Vardy, *Some designs of Mr. Inigo Jones and Mr. William Kent*	1	1744 London	1796	—
141. Wallis, *The complete modern joiner*	1	2d ed. 1772 London	1797?	—
143. Ware, *Designs of Inigo Jones*	1	ca.1735 London	1754	HP85
145. Wood, *A series of plans, for cottages*	1	1781? London	1800	—
146. Wren, *Parentalia*	1	1750 London	1770	—
147. Wrighte, *Grotesque architecture*	1	1767 London	1800	—

APPENDIX B

Treatises Listed by Date of Earliest American Catalogue Reference

1693 Fréart, *Parallele de l'architecture antique et de la moderne* (Paris, 1650); *Parallel of the antient architecture with the modern* (London, 1664)
Jones (I.), *The most notable antiquity of Great Britain* (London, 1655)

1723 Alberti, *L'architettura* (Florence, 1550)
Perrault (Claude), *Ordonnance des cinq especes de colones* (Paris, 1683); *A treatise of the five orders of columns in architecture* (London, 1708)

1734 Mandey, *Mellificum mensionis* (London, 1682)

1741 *The builder's dictionary* (London, 1734)
Campbell, *Vitruvius Britannicus* (London, 1715-71)
Gauger, *La mechanique du feu* (Paris 1713); *Fires improved* (London, 1715)
Leoni, *The architecture of A. Palladio* (London, 1715-19)
Price, *The British carpenter* (London, 1733)

1743 [Neve], *The city and countrey purchaser* (London, 1703)

1746 Langley, *Practical geometry* (London, 1726)

1754 Gibbs, *Rules for drawing the several parts of architecture* (London, 1732)
Hoppus, *The gentleman's and builder's repository* (London, 1737)
Langley, *The city and country builder's, and workman's treasury of designs* (London, 1740)

Salmon, *Palladio Londinensis* (London, 1734)
Swan, *The British architect* (London, 1745)
Ware, *Designs of Inigo Jones* (London, ca. 1735)
Ware, *The four books of Andrea Palladio's architecture* (London, 1738)

1755 Keay, *The practical measurer* (London, 1718)
Salmon, *The London and country builder's vade mecum* (London, 1745)

1757 Castell, *The villas of the ancients* (London, 1728)
Halfpenny, *Useful architecture* (London, 1752)

1758 Leybourn, *The mirror of architecture* (London, 1669)

1759 Halfpenny, *The modern builder's assistant* (London, 1742)
Le Clerc, *Traité d'architecture* (Paris, 1714); *A treatise of archtecture* (London, 1723-24)

1760 Coggeshall, *The art of measuring*, 5th ed. (London, 1732)
Decker, *Chinese architecture* (London, 1759)
Gibbs, *A book of architecture* (London, 1728)
Halfpenny, *The country gentleman's pocket companion* (London, 1753)
Halfpenny, *Practical architecture* (London, 1724?)
Halfpenny, *Rural architecture in the Gothic taste* (London, 1752)
Halfpenny, *Twenty new designs of Chinese lattice* (London, 1750)
Hoppus, *Practical measuring* (London, 1736)
Langley, *The builder's chest-book* (London, 1727)
Langley, *The builder's jewel* (London, 1741)
Langley, *The workman's golden rule* (London, 1750)
Morris, *Architecture improved* (London, 1755)
Morris, *Select architecture* (London, 1755)
Moxon, *The theory and practice of architecture; or, Vitruvius and Vignola abridged*, 5th ed. (London, 1702-03)

Over, *Ornamental architecture* (London, 1758)
Pain, *The builder's companion* (London, 1758)
Rowland, *Compleat tables for measuring round and square timber* (London, 1745)
Salmon, *The builder's guide* (London, 1736)
Salmon, *The country builder's estimator* (London, 1737)
Swan, *A collection of designs in architecture* (London, 1757)
Vitruvius, *De architectura* (Rome, 1483-90)

1761 Langley, *The builder's compleat assistant* (London, 1738)

1762 Garret, *Designs and estimates, of farm houses* (London, 1747)
Halfpenny, *Chinese and Gothic architecture* (London, 1752)
Halfpenny, *A new and compleat system of architecture* (London, 1749)
Halfpenny, *Twelve beautiful designs for farm-houses* (London, 1750)
Hawney, *The compleat measurer* (London, 1717)
Jores, *A new book of iron work* (London, 1759)
Langley, *The builder's director* (London, 1747)
Robinson, *Proportional architecture* (London, 1733)

1764 Oakley, *The magazine of architecture* (Westminster, 1730)
Ralph, *A critical review of the publick buildings, statues and ornaments in, and about London and Westminster* (London, 1734)
Several prospects of the most noted publick buildings, in and about the city of London (London, 1724)
Smith, *The carpenter's companion* (London, 1733)
Ware, *A complete body of architecture* (London, 1756)

1765 Langley, *Ancient masonry* (London, 1736)
Leoni, *The architecture of Leon Battista Alberti* (London, 1726)

1766 Lightholer, *The gentleman and farmer's architect* (London, 1762)

Architectural Books in Early America

1767 [Halfpenny], *The builder's pocket companion* (London, 1728)

1768 Espie, *Maniere de rendre toutes sortes d'édifices incombustibles* (Paris, 1754); *The manner of securing all sorts of buildings from fire* (London, 1755)

1770 Chambers, *Designs of Chinese buildings* (London, 1757)
Wren, *Parentalia* (London, 1750)

1771 Langley, *Gothick architecture* (London, 1747)
Lock & Copland, *A new book of ornaments* (London, 1752)
Miller, *Andrea Palladio's Elements of architecture* (London, 1748)
Swan, *Designs in carpentry; The carpenter's complete instructor* (London, 1759)

1772 Langley, *The London prices of bricklayer materials* (London, 1748)

1773 Crunden, *Convenient and ornamental architecture* (London, 1767)
Jones (W.), *The gentlemens or builders companion* (London?, ca. 1735?)
Morris, *Lectures on architecture* (London, 1734-36)
Pain, *The builder's pocket-treasure* (London, 1763)
Riou, *Short principles for the architecture of stone-bridges* (London, 1760)
Swan, *Designs for chimnies; upwards of one hundred and fifty new designs* (London, 1765)

1775 Adam, *The works in architecture* (London, 1773-1822)

1783 Laugier, *Essai sur l'architecture* (Paris, 1753); *An essay on architecture* (London, 1755)
Perrault (Claude), *Architecture générale de Vitruve* (Amsterdam, 1681)

Architectural Books in Early America

1785 Félebien, *Des principes de l'architecture* (Paris, 1676)
Ferrerio, *Palazzi di Roma* (Rome, 1655)
Vignola, *Regola delli cinque ordini d'architettura* (Rome or Venice, 1563?)

1787 [Norman], *The town and country builder's assistant* (Boston, 1786)
Pain, *The carpenter's and joiner's repository* (London, 1778)
Pain, *The carpenter's pocket directory* (London 1781)
The rudiments of architecture (Edinburgh, 1772)

1789 Anderson, *A practical treatise on chimneys* (Edinburgh, 1776)
Peacock, *Οἰκίδια, or, nutshells* (London, 1785)
Riou, *The Grecian orders of architecture* (London, 1768)
Semple, *A treatise on building in water* (Dublin, 1776)

1790 Chambers, *A treatise on civil architecture* (London, 1759)
Hodgson, *The complete measurer*, 7th ed. (Dublin, 1779)
Palladio, *I quattro libri dell'architettura* (Venice, 1570)
Rusconi, *Della architettura* (Venice, 1590)
Serlio, *Tutte l'opere d'architettura* (Venice, 1584)
Soane, *Designs in architecture* (London, 1778)

1791 Hutton, *Principles of bridges* (Newcastle, 1772)

1792 Pain, *The practical builder* (London, 1774)

1793 *The builder's price-book* (London, 1785)
Crunden, *The joyner and cabinet-maker's darling* (London, 1765)
Kent, *The designs of Inigo Jones* (London, 1727)
Pain, *Pain's British Palladio* (London, 1786)
Robinson, *Gentleman and builder's director* (London, 1774)

1794 Good, *Measuring made easy* (London, 1719)
Pool, *Views of the most remarkable public buildings, monuments and other edifices in the city of Dublin*

(Dublin, 1780)
Smeaton, *Narrative of the building . . . of the Edystone lighthouse* (London, 1791)
Soane, *Plan, elevations, and sections of buildings* (London, 1788)

1795 Morrison, *Useful and ornamental designs in architecture* (Dublin, 1793)
Perrault (Charles), *Parallele des anciens et des modernes* (Paris, 1688-97)
Richards, *The first book of architecture, by Andrea Palladio* (London, 1663)

1796 Columbani, *A new book of ornaments* (London, 1775)
Columbani, *Variety of capitals, freezes, and corniches* (London, 1776)
Darly, *A compleat body of architecture* (London, 1773)
Halfpenny, *The art of sound building* (London, 1725)
Halfpenny, *Rural architecture in the Chinese taste*, 2d ed. (London, 1752)
Oakley, *Every man a compleat builder* (London, 1738)
Pain, *The practical house carpenter* (London, 1788)
Vardy, *Some designs of Mr. Inigo Jones and Mr. William Kent* (London, 1744)

1797 [Crunden], *The carpenter's companion for Chinese railing and gates* (London, 1765)
Designs for chimney-pieces (London, 1793)
Designs for shop-fronts and door-cases (London, 179-?)
Manwaring, *The carpenter's compleat guide* (London, 1765)
Middleton, *Picturesque and architectural views* (London, 1793)
Nicolson, *The carpenter's new guide* (London, 1793)
Nicholson, *The student's instructor in drawing and working the five orders of architecture* (London, 1795)
Paine, *Plans, elevations and sections of noblemen and gentlemen's houses* (London, 1767-83)

Wallis, *The complete modern joiner*, 2d ed. (London, 1772)

1798 *The carpenters rules of work in the town of Boston* (Boston, 1774)
Desgodets, *Les édifices antiques de Rome* (Paris, 1682); *The ancient buildings of Rome* (London, 1795)
Plaw, *Ferme ornée* (London, 1795)
Sousa Coutinho, *Plans, elevations, sections and views of the church of Batalha* (London, 1795)

1799 Benjamin, *The country builder's assistant* (Greenfield, Mass., 1797)

1800 Laing, *Hints for dwellings* (London, 1800)
[Middleton], *Decorations for parks and gardens* (London, 1800?)
Miller, *The country gentleman's architect* (London, 1787)
Nicholson, *The carpenter and joiner's assistant* (London, 1792?)
Ornamental iron work (London, 1800?)
Ornaments displayed (London, 178-?)
Plaw, *Sketches for country houses* (London, 1800)
The principles of drawing ornaments made easy (London, 1780)
Rawlins, *Familiar architecture* (London, 1768)
The rudiments of ancient architecture (London, 1789)
Wood, *A series of plans, for cottages* (London, 1781?)
Wrighte, *Grotesque architecture* (London, 1767)

APPENDIX C

Treatises Listed Alphabetically by
Individual Library or Firm

	Earliest catalogue record
Albany, N.Y., Albany Library	
Halfpenny, *Useful architecture*	1793
Allen, Thomas (fl. 1785-99), bookseller, New York, N.Y.	
Hawney, *The compleat measurer*	1792
Hoppus, *Practical measuring*	1792
Langley, *The builder's jewel*	1792
Price, *The British carpenter*	1792
Salmon, *Palladio Londinensis*	1792
Arnold, Benedict (1741-1801), druggist & bookseller, New Haven, Conn.	
Salmon, *Palladio Londinensis*	1763?
Baltimore, Md., Library Company	
Chambers, *A treatise on civil architecture*	1798
Desgodets, *The ancient buildings of Rome*	1798
Leoni, *The architecture of A. Palladio*	1797
Middleton, *Picturesque and architectural views for cottages, farm houses, and country villas*	1797
Morrison, *Useful and ornamental designs in architecture*	1798
Pain, *The carpenter's and joiner's repository*	1798
Pain, *Pain's British Palladio*	1797
Paine (James), *Plans, elevations, and sections*	1797
[Peacock], *Οἰκίδια, or, nutshells*	1798
Price, *The British carpenter*	1798
Semple, *A treatise on building in water*	1797

Architectural Books in Early America

Smeaton, *A narrative of the building and a description of the construction of the Edystone lighthouse*	1798
Soane, *Designs in architecture*	1798
Sousa Coutinho, *Plans, elevations, sections, and views of the church of Batalha*	1798

Beers, Isaac (1742?-1813), bookseller, New Haven, Conn.

Hoppus, *Practical measuring*	1791
Langley, *The builder's jewel*	1791
[Norman], *The town and country builder's assistant*	1791
Price, *The British carpenter*	1791
Salmon, *The London and country builder's vade mecum*	1791
Swan, *A collection of designs in architecture*	1791

Bell, Robert (1731?-84), bookseller, Philadelphia, Pa.

The builder's dictionary	1783
Crunden, *Convenient and ornamental architecture*	1773
Halfpenny, *The modern builder's assistant*	1773
Hoppus, *The gentleman's and builder's repository*	1783
Jores, *A new book of iron work*	1770
Langley, *Ancient masonry*	1773
Langley, *The builder's compleat assistant*	1773
Langley, *The builder's director*	1783
Langley, *The builder's jewel*	1773
Langley, *The city and country builder's, and workman's treasury of designs*	1773
Langley, *The workman's golden rule*	1783
Laugier, *Essai sur l'architecture*	1783
Le Clerc, *A treatise of architecture*	1783
Lightoler, *The gentleman and farmer's architect*	1783
Morris, *Architecture improved*	1783
Over, *Ornamental architecture*	1783
Perrault (Claude), *Architecture générale de Vitruve*	1783
Salmon, *Palladio Londinensis*	1783
Swan, *The British architect*	1783
Swan, *Designs in carpentry; The carpenter's complete assistant*	1773

Architectural Books in Early America

Ware, *The four books of Andrea Palladio's architecture*   1783

Blake, William Pynson (1769-1820), bookseller, Boston, Mass.
    Halfpenny, *A new and complete system of architecture*   1793
    Langley, *The builder's jewel*   1793
    Langley, *The city and country builder's, and
        workman's treasury of designs*   1793
    Leoni, *The architecture of A. Palladio*   1793
    Miller, *Andrea Palladio's Elements of architecture*   1793
    [Norman], *The town and country builder's assistant*   1793
    Pain, *The builder's companion*   1793
    Pain, *The builder's pocket-treasure*   1793
    Riou, *The Grecian orders of architecture*   1793
    Swan, *The British architect*   1793

Blake, William Pynson (1769-1820), & Lemuel (1775-1861), booksellers, Boston, Mass.
    Carpenters' rules of work in the town of Boston   1798
    Designs for chimney-pieces   1798
    Langley, *The builder's jewel*   1798
    [Norman], *The town and country builder's assistant*   1798
    Pain, *The builder's pocket-treasure*   1798
    Pain, *The carpenter's pocket director*   1798
    Pain, *The practical builder*   1798
    Pain, *The practical house carpenter*   1798
    Swan, *The British architect*   1798
    Swan, *Designs in carpentry;The carpenter's complete
        instructor*   1798

Boston, Mass., broadside, September 30, 1766
    Halfpenny, *A new and compleat system of architecture*   1766
    Lightoler, *The gentleman and farmer's architect*   1766
    Pain, *The builder's companion*   1766

Bradford, Thomas (1745-1838), bookseller, Philadelphia, Pa.
    Columbani, *A new book of ornaments*   1796
    Columbani, *Variety of capitals, freezes, and corniches*   1796

Darly, *A compleat body of architecture*	1796
Gibbs, *Rules for drawing the several parts of architecture*	1796
Halfpenny, *The art of sound building*	1796
Halfpenny, *The modern builder's assistant*	1796
Halfpenny, *A new and compleat system of architecture*	1796
Halfpenny, *Practical architecture*	1796
Halfpenny, *Rural architecture in the Chinese taste*	1796
Halfpenny, *Rural architecture in the Gothic taste*	1796
Halfpenny, *Useful architecture*	1796
Hawney, *The compleat measurer*	1796
Kent, *The designs of Inigo Jones*	1796
Leoni, *The architecture of A. Palladio*	1796
Lightoler, *The gentleman and farmer's architect*	1796
Lock & Copland, *A new book of ornaments*	1796
Oakley, *Every man a compleat builder*	1796
Swan, *A collection of designs in architecture*	1796
Swan, *Designs in carpentry; The carpenter's complete instructor*	1796
Vardy, *Some designs of Mr. Inigo Jones and Mr. Wm. Kent*	1796

Bradford, William (1719-91), auctioneer, Philadelphia, Pa.

The builder's dictionary	1760?
Langley, *The city and country builder's, and workman's treasury of designs*	1760?
Salmon, *Palladio Londinensis*	1760?

Bradford, William (1719-91), & Thomas (1745-1838), booksellers, Philadelphia, Pa.

Hawney, *The compleat measurer*	1767?

Bristol, R.I., Potter Library Company

Pain, *The practical house carpenter*	1800

Burlington, N.J., Library Company

Leybourn, *The mirror of architecture*	1758

Architectural Books in Early America

Cambell, Duncan (fl. 1693-95), bookseller, Boston, Mass.
[The library of Rev. Samuel Lee (1625-91)]
    Fréart, *A parallel of the antient architecture with the modern*   1693
    Jones (I.), *The most notable antiquity of Great Britain*   1693

Campbell, Robert (d. 1800), bookseller, Philadelphia, Pa.
    Hawney, *The compleat measurer*   1790?
    Hoppus, *Practical measuring*   1791
    [Norman], *The town and country builder's assistant*   1791
    Pain, *The builder's pocket-treasure*   1797
    Pain, *The practical builder*   1794
    Swan, *The British architect*   1794

Campbell, Samuel (1763?-1836), bookseller, New York, N.Y.
    Good, *Measuring made easy*   1794
    Hoppus, *Practical measuring*   1787
    Middleton, *Picturesque and architectural views for cottages, farm houses, and country villas*   1798
    [Norman], *The town and country builder's assistant*   1787
    Pain, *The builder's pocket-treasure*   1798
    Pain, *The practical builder*   1794
    Price, *The British carpenter*   1787
    The rudiments of architecture   1787
    Semple, *A treatise on building in water*   1798
    Swan, *The British architect*   1798
    Swan, *Designs in carpentry; The carpenter's complete instructor*   1787

Carey, Mathew (1760-1839), bookseller, Philadelphia, Pa.
    Anderson, *A practical treatise on chimneys*   1793
    The builder's dictionary   1794
    Hawney, *The compleat measurer*   1794
    Hoppus, *Practical measuring*   1794
    Hutton, *Principles of bridges*   1794
    Langley, *The builder's jewel*   1794
    [Norman], *The town and country builder's assistant*   1794

Pain, *The carpenter's pocket directory*   1798
Pain, *The practical builder*   1794
Pool, *Views of the most remarkable public buildings, monuments and other edifices in the city of Dublin*   1794

Caritat, Louis Alexis Hocquet de (b. 1752), bookseller, New York, N.Y.
     Morris, *Lectures on architecture*   1799
     Price, *The British carpenter*   1799

Charleston, S.C., Library Society
     The builder's dictionary   1770
     Chambers, *Designs of Chinese buildings*   1770
     Fréart, *A parallel of the antient architecture with the modern*   1770
     Gibbs, *A book of architecture*   1770
     Gibbs, *Rules for drawing the several parts of architecture*   1770
     Jones (I.), *The most notable antiquity of Great Britain*   1770
     Leoni, *The architecture of A. Palladio*   1770
     Pain, *The builder's companion*   1770
     Price, *The British carpenter*   1770
     Wren, *Parentalia*   1770

Childs, Francis (1763-1830), & Company, booksellers, New York, N.Y.
     Hawney, *The compleat measurer*   1793
     Hoppus, *Practical measuring*   1793

Clarkson, Matthew (1758-1825), & Ebenezer Hazard (1744-1817), estate administrators, Philadelphia, Pa.
     Félebièn, *Des principes de l'architecture*   1785
     Vignola, *Reigle des cinq ordres d'architecture (?)*   1785

Cox, Edward (fl. 1766-78), & Edward Berry (fl. 1766-72), booksellers, Boston, Mass.
     Garret, *Designs, and estimates, of farm houses*   1772?
     Halfpenny, *Twelve beautiful designs for farm-houses*   1772?

Architectural Books in Early America

Hawney, *The compleat measurer*	1772?
Hoppus, *Practical measuring*	1772?
Langley, *The builder's compleat assistant*	1772?
Langley, *The builder's director*	1772?
Langley, *The builder's jewel*	1772?
Langley, *The London prices of bricklayers materials and works*	1772?
Langley, *The workman's golden rule*	1772?
Swan, *The British architect*	1772?
Swan, *A collection of designs in architecture*	1772?

Cox, Thomas (fl. 1733-44), London bookseller, Boston, Mass.
Mandey, *Mellificum mensionis*	1734

Crukshank, Joseph (1746?-1836), bookseller, Philadelphia, Pa.
Hawney, *The compleat measurer*	1789

Dabney, John (1752-1819), bookseller, Salem, Mass.
Langley, *The builder's jewel*	1794
Pain, *The practical builder*	1794

Dunlap, William (d. 1779), bookseller, Philadelphia, Pa.
Halfpenny, *Practical architecture*	1760
Hoppus, *Practical measuring*	1760
Price, *The British carpenter*	1760
Salmon, *The London and country builder's vade mecum*	1760

Fenno, John Ward (1778-1802), bookseller, New York, N.Y.
Columbani, *A new book of ornaments*	1800
Columbani, *Variety of capitals, freezes, and corniches*	1800
Crunden, *Convenient and ornamental architecture*	1800
Designs for chimney-pieces	1800
Laing, *Hints for dwellings*	1800
Langley, *The builder's compleat assistant*	1800
Langley, *The builder's director*	1800
[Middleton], *Decorations for parks and gardens*	1800
Miller, *The country gentleman's architect*	1800

Nicholson, *The carpenter and joiner's assistant*   1800
Nicholson, *The student's instructor in drawing and
   working the five orders of architecture*   1800
Ornamental iron work   1800
Ornaments displayed   1800
Pain, *The builder's pocket-treasure*   1800
Pain, *The carpenter's and joiner's repository*   1800
Pain, *The carpenter's pocket directory*   1800
Pain, *Pain's British Palladio*   1800
Pain, *The practical builder*   1800
Pain, *The practical house carpenter*   1800
Plaw, *Sketches for country houses, villas, and
   rural dwellings*   1800
The principles of drawing ornaments made easy   1800
Rawlins, *Familiar architecture*   1800
The rudiments of ancient architecture   1800
Soane, *Designs in architecture*   1800
Wood, *A series of plans, for cottages*   1800
Wrighte, *Grotesque architecture*   1800

Gaine, Hugh (1726-1807), bookseller, New York, N.Y.
   Langley, *The builder's jewel*   1771
   Price, *The British carpenter*   1787
   Swan, *The British architect*   1787

Guild, Benjamin (1749-92), bookseller, Boston, Mass.
   Adam, *The works in architecture*   1787?
   Gibbs, *A book of architecture*   1787?
   Halfpenny, *A new and compleat system of architecture*   1787?
   Langley, *The builder's compleat assistant*   1787?
   Langley, *The builder's jewel*   1787?
   [Norman], *The town and country builder's assistant*   1787?
   Pain, *The builder's pocket-treasure*   1789
   Pain, *The carpenter's and joiner's repository*   1787?
   Riou, *The Grecian orders of architecture*   1789
   Rowland, *Compleat tables for measuring round and
      square timber*   1787?

Architectural Books in Early America

Swan, *A collection of designs in architecture*	1789
Ware, *The four books of Andrea Palladio's architecture*	1789

Hall, David (1714-72), bookseller, Philadelphia, Pa.

The builder's dictionary	1754
Espie, *The manner of securing all sorts of buildings from fire*	1768?
Gibbs, *A book of architecture*	1763?
Gibbs, *Rules for drawing the several parts of architecture*	1754
[Halfpenny], *The builder's pocket companion*	1767
Halfpenny, *The modern builder's assistant*	1760?
Halfpenny, *Practical architecture*	1760?
Hawney, *The compleat measurer*	1763?
Hoppus, *The gentleman's and builder's repository*	1754
Keay, *The practical measurer*	1763?
Langley, *The builder's compleat assistant*	1761?
Langley, *The builder's jewel*	1760?
Langley, *The city and country builder's and workman's treasury of designs*	1754
Langley, *The workman's golden rule*	1763?
Pain, *The builder's companion*	1763?
Price, *The British carpenter*	1754
Rowland, *Compleat tables for measuring round and square timber*	1760?
Salmon, *The country builder's estimator*	1763?
Salmon, *The London and country builder's vade mecum*	1763?
Salmon, *Palladio Londinensis*	1754
Swan, *The British architect*	1754
Swan, *A collection of designs in architecture*	1763?
Ware, *Designs of Inigo Jones and others*	1754
Ware, *The four books of Andrea Palladio's architecture*	1763?

Hall, William (1752-1834), bookseller, Philadelphia, Pa.

Hawney, *The compleat measurer*	1774?
Hoppus, *The gentleman's and builder's repository*	1774?
Langley, *The builder's jewel*	1774?
Price, *The British carpenter*	1774?

Architectural Books in Early America

Salmon, *Palladio Londinensis*	1774?
Swan, *A collection of designs in architecture*	1774?
Ware, *The four books of Andrea Palladio's architecture*	1774?

Hanover, N.H., Hanover Bookstore
Benjamin, *The country builder's assistant*	1799
Pain, *The builder's pocket-treasure*	1799
Pain, *The practical builder*	1799
Pain, *The practical house carpenter*	1799

Harris, Thaddeus Mason (1768-1842), librarian, Harvard College
Robinson, *Gentleman and builder's director*	1793

Harvard College Library, Cambridge, Mass.
Alberti, *L'architettura*	1723
Campbell, *Vitruvius Britannicus*	1790
Chambers, *A treatise on civil architecture*	1790
Leoni, *The architecture of A. Palladio*	1790
Palladio, *I quattro libri dell'architettura*	1790
Perrault (Claude), *A treatise of the five orders of columns in architecture*	1723
Rusconi, *Della architettura*	1790
Serlio, *Tutte l'opera d'architettura*	1790
Vignola, *Regola delli cinque ordini d'architettura*	1790
Vitruvius, *Di architecturi*	1790

Hudson, Barzillai (1741-1823), & George Goodwin (1757-1844), booksellers, Hartford, Conn.
Pain, *The carpenter's pocket directory*	1797
Pain, *Pain's British Palladio*	1797
[Peacock], *Οικίδια, or, nutshells*	1797

Knox, Henry (1750-1806), bookseller, Boston, Mass.
Gibbs, *A book of architecture*	1773
Halfpenny, *A new and compleat system of architecture*	1773
Hoppus, *Practical measuring*	1773

Architectural Books in Early America

Jones (W.), *The gentlemens or builders companion*	1773
Langley, *The builder's chest-book*	1773
Langley, *The builder's director*	1773
Langley, *The builder's jewel*	1773
Langley, *The city and country builder's, and workman's treasury of designs*	1773
Morris, *Lectures on architecture*	1773
Pain, *The builder's companion*	1773
Pain, *The builder's pocket-treasure*	1773
Price, *The British carpenter*	1773
Riou, *Short principles for the architecture of stone-bridges*	1773
Salmon, *The country builder's estimator*	1773
Salmon, *Palladio Londinensis*	1773
Swan, *Designs for chimnies*	1773

Lancaster, Pa., Juliana Library Company

The builder's dictionary	1766
Price, *The British carpenter*	1766

Larkin, Ebenezer (1767-1813), bookseller, Boston, Mass.

The builder's price-book	1793
Crunden, *Convenient and ornamental architecture*	1793
Crunden, *The joyner and cabinet-maker's darling*	1793
Langley, *The builder's compleat assistant*	1793
Langley, *The builder's jewel*	1793
Nicholson, *The student's instructor in drawing and working the five orders of architecture*	1798
[Norman], *The town and country builder's assistant*	1793
Pain, *The builder's pocket-treasure*	1798
Pain, *The carpenter's pocket directory*	1793
Pain, *The practical builder*	1793
Pain, *Pain's British Palladio*	1793
Swan, *A collection of designs in architecture*	1798

Larkin, Samuel (1773-1849), bookseller, Portsmouth, N.H.

Pain, *The builder's pocket-treasure*	1796
Pain, *Pain's British Palladio*	1796

Pain, *The practical builder* 1796
Pain, *The practical house carpenter* 1796

Martin, William, bookseller, Boston, Mass.
    Ware, *A complete body of architecture* 1786

Mein, John (fl. 1760-75), bookseller, Boston, Mass.
    Hawney, *The compleat measurer* 1765
    Hoppus, *Practical measuring* 1765
    Langley, *The builder's director* 1766
    Langley, *The builder's jewel* 1765
    Salmon, *Palladio Londinensis* 1765
    Smith, *The carpenter's companion* 1766

Moreau de Saint-Méry, Médéric Louis Elie (1750-1819), & Company, booksellers, Philadelphia, Pa.
    Fréart, *Parallele de l'architecture antique et de la moderne* 1795

Nancrede, Paul Joseph Guérard de (1760-1841), bookseller, Boston, Mass.
    Columbani, *A new book of ornaments* 1798
    Langley, *The builder's jewel* 1796
    Pain, *The practical builder* 1796
    Pain, *The practical house carpenter* 1796

Newport, R.I., Redwood Library
    The following books were purchased by John Thomlinson in London in 1748 for Abraham Redwood. The Red-wood Library opened in 1750. See McCorison, ed. *The 1764 Catalogue of the Red-wood Library Company at New-port, Rhode Island* (New Haven, 1965).
    The builder's dictionary 1764
    Gauger, *Fires improved* 1764
    Oakley, *The magazine of architecture* 1764
    Price, *The British carpenter* 1764
    Ralph, *A critical review* 1764

Architectural Books in Early America

    Salmon, *Palladio Londinensis* — 1764
    Smith, *The carpenter's companion* — 1764
    Ware, *The four books of Andrea Palladio's architecture* — 1764

New York, N.Y., Corporation of the City of New York Library
    Fréart, *A parallel of the antient architecture with the modern* — 1766

New York, N.Y., Society Library
    The builder's dictionary — 1792
    Campbell, *Vitruvius Britannicus* — 1758
    Gauger, *Fires improved* — 1758
    Gibbs, *A book of architecture* — 1789
    Gibbs, *Rules for drawing the several parts of architecture* — 1789
    Halfpenny, *Useful architecture* — 1758
    Hoppus, *The gentleman's and builder's repository* — 1773
    Hutton, *Principles of bridges* — 1791
    Langley, *The builder's jewel* — 1792
    Pain, *The carpenter's and joiner's repository* — 1791
    Price, *The British carpenter* — 1789
    Riou, *Short principles for the architecture of stone-bridges* — 1793
    Semple, *A treatise on building in water* — 1789
    Swan, *The British architect* — 1792
    Ware, *The four books of Andrea Palladio's architecture* — 1791

Noel, Garrat (fl. 1752-75), bookseller, New York, N.Y.
    Garret, *Designs, and estimates, of farm houses* — 1762
    Halfpenny, *Chinese and Gothic architecture* — 1762
    Halfpenny, *The modern builder's assistant* — 1759
    Halfpenny, *A new and compleat system of architecture* — 1762
    Halfpenny, *Useful architecture* — 1762
    Hoppus, *Practical measuring* — 1762
    Jores, *A new book of iron work* — 1762
    Keay, *The practical measurer* — 1755
    Langley, *The builder's director* — 1762
    Le Clerc, *A treatise of architecture* — 1759

Morris, *Architecture improved* 1762
Morris, *Select architecture* 1762
Over, *Ornamental architecture* 1762
Pain, *The builder's companion* 1762
Price, *The British carpenter* 1759
Robinson, *Proportional architecture* 1762
Salmon, *The London and country builder's vade mecum* 1755
Swan, *A collection of designs in architecture* 1762

Noel, Garrat (fl. 1752-75), & Ebenezer Hazard (1744-1817), booksellers, New York, N.Y.
Garret, *Designs, and estimates, of farm houses* 1771
Halfpenny, *The country gentleman's pocket companion* 1771
Halfpenny, *A new and compleat system of architecture* 1771
Halfpenny, *Useful architecture* 1771
Hawney, *The compleat measurer* 1771
Jores, *A new book of iron work* 1771
Langley, *The builder's compleat assistant* 1771
Langley, *The builder's director* 1771
Langley, *Gothick architecture* 1771
Lightoler, *The gentleman and farmer's architect* 1771
Lock & Copland, *A new book of ornaments* 1771
Miller, *Andrea Palladio's Elements of architecture* 1771
Morris, *Architecture improved* 1771
Over, *Ornamental architecture* 1771
Pain, *The builder's companion* 1771
Price, *The British carpenter* 1771
Swan, *The British architect* 1771
Swan, *A collection of designs in architecture* 1771
Swan, *Designs in carpentry; The carpenter's complete instructor* 1771

Payne, Jonas, & Philip Hearn, booksellers, Savannah, Ga.
Hoppus, *Practical measuring* 1790
Price, *The British carpenter* 1790

Architectural Books in Early America

Philadelphia, Pa., Association Library Company
[Neve], *The city and country purchaser* 1765
Swan, *A collection of designs in architecture* 1765

Philadelphia, Pa., Library Company
Adam, *The works in architecture* 1775
Anderson, *A practical treatise on chimneys* 1789
The builder's dictionary 1741
Campbell, *Vitruvius Britannicus* 1741
Castell, *The villas of the ancients illustrated* 1757
Crunden, *Convenient and ornamental architecture* 1794
Espie, *The manner of securing all sorts of buildings from fire* 1789
Gauger, *Fires improved* 1741
Gibbs, *A book of architecture* 1775
Gibbs, *Rules for drawing the several parts of architecture* 1770
Halfpenny, *Useful architecture* 1757
Jones (I.), *The most notable antiquity of Great Britain* 1757
Kent, *The designs of Inigo Jones* 1793
Langley, *Ancient masonry* 1770
Langley, *Practical geometry* 1746
Leoni, *The architecture of A. Palladio* 1741
Leoni, *The architecture of Leon Battista Alberti* 1770
[Neve], *The city and country purchaser* 1770
Pain, *Pain's British Palladio* 1794
[Peacock], *Οἰκίδια, or, nutshells* 1789
Perrault (Claude), *A treatise of the five orders of columns in architecture* 1770
Plaw, *Ferme ornée* 1798
Price, *The British carpenter* 1741
Salmon, *Palladio Londinensis* 1770
Semple, *A treatise on building in water* 1794
Several prospects of the most noted publick buildings, in and about the city of London 1764
Smeaton, *Narrative of the building and a description of the construction of the Edystone lighthouse* 1794
Soane, *Designs in architecture* 1794

Architectural Books in Early America

Soane, *Plans, elevations, and sections of buildings*	1794
Swan, *The British architect*	1775
Swan, *A collection of designs in architecture*	1770
Ware, *A complete body of architecture*	1764
Ware, *The four books of Andrea Palladio's architecture*	1770

Philadelphia, Pa., Loganian Library

Gauger, *La mecanique du feu*	1760
Langley, *The city and country builder's, and workman's treasury of designs*	1795
Moxon, *The theory and practice of architecture; or, Vitruvius and Vignola abridged*	1760
[Neve], *The city and country purchaser*	1760
Perrault (Charles), *Parallele des anciens et des modernes*	1795
Richards, *The first book of architecture, by Andrea Palladio*	1795
Vitruvius, *De architectura*	1760

Philadelphia, Pa., Union Library Company

Hawney, *The compleat measurer*	1765
Langley, *Ancient masonry*	1765
Leoni, *The architecture of Leon Battista Alberti*	1765
[Neve], *The city and country purchaser*	1765
Perrault (Claude), *A treatise of the five orders of columns in architecture*	1754
Price, *The British carpenter*	1754
Swan, *A collection of designs in architecture*	1765
Ware, *The four books of Andrea Palladio's architecture*	1754

Prichard, William (fl. 1782-1809), bookseller, Philadelphia, Pa.

Ferrerio, *Palazzi di Roma*	1785
Hawney, *The compleat measurer*	1789
Langley, *The builder's jewel*	1785
Price, *The British carpenter*	1785

Providence, R.I., Providence Library

Hawney, *The compleat measurer*	1768

Architectural Books in Early America

    Langley, *The builder's compleat assistant*   1768
    Salmon, *Palladio Londinensis*   1768

Rhode Island College Library [Brown University], Providence, R.I.
    Gauger, *Fires improved*   1793
    Mandey, *Mellificum mensionis*   1793

Rice, Henry (d. 1804), & Company, booksellers, Philadelphia, Pa.
    Hawney, *The compleat measurer*   1789?
    Hodgson, *The complete measurer*   1790?
    Langley, *The builder's jewel*   1790?
    Price, *The British carpenter*   1790?
    Semple, *A treatise on building in water*   1790?

Rice, Henry (d. 1804), & Patrick (fl. 1792-1804), booksellers, Philadelphia, Pa.
    Hodgson, *The complete measurer*   1795
    Hoppus, *Practical measuring*   1795
    Langley, *The builder's jewel*   1795
    Morrison, *Useful and ornamental designs in architecture*   1795
    [Norman], *The town and country builder's assistant*   1795
    Pain, *The practical builder*   1795
    Price, *The British carpenter*   1795
    Semple, *A treatise on building in water*   1795
    Swan, *The British architect*   1795

Rivington, James (1724-1802), bookseller, New York, N.Y., & Philadelphia, Pa.
    The builder's dictionary   1760
    Coggeshall, *The art of measuring*   1760
    Decker, *Chinese architecture*   1760
    Gibbs, *A book of architecture*   1760
    Gibbs, *Rules for drawing the several parts of architecture*   1760
    Halfpenny, *The country gentleman's pocket companion*   1760
    Halfpenny, *The modern builder's assistant*   1760

Halfpenny, *Rural architecture in the Gothic taste*	1760
Halfpenny, *Twenty new designs of Chinese lattice*	1760
Halfpenny, *Useful architecture*	1760
Hoppus, *The gentleman's and builder's repository*	1760
Langley, *The builder's chest-book*	1760
Langley, *The builder's jewel*	1760
Langley, *The city and country builder's, and workman's treasury of designs*	1760
Langley, *The workman's golden rule*	1760
Morris, *Architecture improved*	1760
Morris, *Select architecture*	1760
Over, *Ornamental architecture*	1760
Pain, *The builder's companion*	1760
Price, *The British carpenter*	1760
Salmon, *The builder's guide*	1760
Salmon, *The country builder's estimator*	1760
Salmon, *The London and country builder's vade mecum*	1760
Salmon, *Palladio Londinensis*	1760
Swan, *A collection of designs in architecture*	1760
Ware, *The four books of Andrea Palladio's architecture*	1760

Rivington, James (1724-1802), & Samuel Brown (fl. 1755-69), booksellers, New York, N.Y., & Philadelphia, Pa.

The builder's dictionary	1762
Coggeshall, *The art of measuring*	1762
Garret, *Designs, and estimates, of farm houses*	1762
Gibbs, *A book of architecture*	1762
Gibbs, *Rules for drawing the several parts of architecture*	1762
Halfpenny, *The country gentleman's pocket companion*	1762
Halfpenny, *The modern builder's assistant*	1762
Halfpenny, *A new and compleat system of architecture*	1762
Halfpenny, *Twelve beautiful designs for farm-houses*	1762
Halfpenny, *Useful architecture*	1762
Hawney, *The compleat measurer*	1762
Hoppus, *The gentleman's and builder's repository*	1762
Jores, *A new book of iron work*	1762
Keay, *The practical measurer*	1762

Langley, *The builder's chest-book*	1762
Langley, *The builder's jewel*	1762
Langley, *The city and country builder's, and workman's treasury of designs*	1762
Langley, *The workman's golden rule*	1762
Morris, *Architecture improved*	1762
Morris, *Select architecture*	1762
Over, *Ornamental architecture*	1762
Pain, *The builder's companion*	1762
Price, *The British carpenter*	1762
Rowland, *Compleat tables for measuring round and square timber*	1762
Salmon, *The builder's guide, and gentleman and trader's assistant*	1762
Salmon, *The country builder's estimator*	1762
Salmon, *The London and country builder's vade mecum*	1762
Salmon, *Palladio Londinensis*	1762
Swan, *A collection of designs in architecture*	1762
Ware, *The four books of Andrea Palladio's architecture*	1762

Ross, Joseph, & George Douglas, booksellers, Petersburgh, Va.

Hoppus, *Practical measuring*	1800
Pool, *Views of the most remarkable public buildings, monuments and other edifices in the city of Dublin*	1800

Russell, Joseph (1734-95), & Samuel Clap (1745-1809), auctioneers, Boston, Mass.

Langley, *The builder's chest-book*	1792

Salem, Mass., Social Library

Le Clerc, *A treatise of architecture*	1797?

Sparhawk, John (1730-1803), bookseller, Philadelphia, Pa.

Hawney, *The compleat measurer*	1774?
Hoppus, *Practical measuring*	1774?
Price, *The British carpenter*	1774?

Architectural Books in Early America

Swan, *The British architect*	1774?
Swan, *A collection of designs in architecture*	1774?
Swan, *Designs in carpentry; The carpenter's complete instructor*	1774?

Spotswood, William (1753?-1805), bookseller, Boston, Mass., & Philadelphia, Pa.

Hodgson, *The complete measurer*	1795
Hoppus, *Practical measuring*	1795
[Norman], *The town and country builder's assistant*	1795
Pain, *The practical builder*	1795
Price, *The British carpenter*	1795
Swan, *The British architect*	1795

Stephens, Thomas (fl. 1793-97), bookseller, Philadelphia, Pa.

Langley, *The London prices of bricklayers materials*	1795
Price, *The British carpenter*	1794

Thomas, Isaiah (1749-1831), bookseller, Worcester, Mass., Boston, Mass., & Albany, N.Y.

Hoppus, *Practical measuring*	1792
[Norman], *The town and country builder's assistant*	1787
Pain, *The carpenter's pocket directory*	1787
Pain, *The practical builder*	1792
Salmon, *The London and country builder's vade mecum*	1792

Thomas, Isaiah (1749-1831), & Ebenezer Turrell Andrews (1766-1851), booksellers, Boston, Mass.

Benjamin, *The country builder's assistant*	1799
The builder's price-book	1793
Crunden, , *Convenient and ornamental architecture*	1793
Crunden, *The joyner and cabinet-maker's darling*	1793
Langley, *The builder's compleat assistant*	1793
Langley, *The builder's jewel*	1793
[Norman], *The town and country builder's assistant*	1793
Pain, *The builder's pocket-treasure*	1799
Pain, *The carpenter's pocket directory*	1793

Architectural Books in Early America

    Pain, *Pain's British Palladio* — 1793
    Pain, *The practical builder* — 1793
    Pain, *The practical house carpenter* — 1799

Thomas, Isaiah (1749-1831), Ebenezer Turrell Andrews (1766-1851), & Obadiah Penniman (1766-1820), booksellers, Albany, N.Y.
    Columbani, *A new book of ornaments* — 1797?
    Crunden, *The joyner and cabinet-maker's darling* — 1797?
    Langley, *The builder's director* — 1797?
    Langley, *The builder's jewel* — 1797?
    Nicholson, *The carpenter's new guide* — 1797?
    [Norman], *The town and country builder's assistant* — 1797?
    Pain, *The builder's pocket-treasure* — 1796
    Pain, *The carpenter's pocket directory* — 1797?
    Pain, *Pain's British Palladio* — 1797?
    Pain, *The practical builder* — 1796
    Pain, *The practical house carpenter* — 1797?
    Soane, *Plans, elevations, and sections of buildings* — 1797?
    Swan, *The British architect* — 1797?

Thomas, Isaiah (1749-1831), Isaiah Thomas, Jr. (1773-1819), & Alexander Thomas (1775-1809), booksellers, Worcester, Mass.
    Hoppus, *Practical measuring* — 1796
    Pain, *The builder's pocket treasure* — 1796
    Pain, *The practical builder* — 1796

West, David (1765-1810), bookseller, Boston, Mass.
    Benjamin, *The country builder's assistant* — 1799
    Crunden, *The joyner and cabinet-maker's darling* — 1793
    Langley, *The builder's compleat assistant* — 1793
    Langley, *The builder's jewel* — 1793
    [Norman], *The town and country builder's assistant* — 1793
    Pain, *The builder's pocket-treasure* — 1799
    Pain, *The carpenter's pocket directory* — 1793
    Pain, *Pain's British Palladio* — 1793

Architectural Books in Early America

Pain, *The practical builder*		1793
Pain, *The practical house carpenter*		1799

West, John (1770-1827), bookseller, Boston, Mass.
Pain, *The builder's pocket-treasure*		1797
Pain, *The practical builder*		1797

White, James (1755-1824), bookseller, Boston, Mass.
[Crunden], *The carpenter's companion for Chinese railing and gates*		1797?
Crunden, *Convenient and ornamental architecture*		1797?
Designs for chimney-pieces		1797?
Designs for shop-fronts and door-cases		1797?
Hoppus, *Practical measuring*		1797?
Manwaring, *The carpenter's compleat guide*		1797?
Nicholson, *The carpenter's new guide*		1797?
Nicholson, *The student's instructor in drawing and working the five orders of architecture*		1797?
Pain, *The builder's pocket-treasure*		1797?
Pain, *Pain's British Palladio*		1797?
Pain, *The carpenter's pocket directory*		1797?
Pain, *The practical builder*		1797?
Pain, *The practical house carpenter*		1797?
Wallis, *The complete modern joiner*		1797?

Yale College Library, New Haven, Conn.
Leoni, *The architecture of A. Palladio*		1743
[Neve], *The city and countrey purchaser*		1743

Young, William (1755-1829), bookseller, Philadelphia, Pa.
Leybourn, *The mirror of architecture*		1786
[Norman], *The town and country builder's assistant*		1792
Swan, *The British architect*		1786
Swan, *A collection of designs in architecture*		1786

APPENDIX D

Libraries and Booksellers Listed in Order of the Size of Their Collections

33 titles
    Philadelphia, Pa., Library Company

30 titles
    Rivington, James (1724-1802), & Samuel Brown (fl. 1755-69), booksellers, New York, N.Y., & Philadelphia, Pa.

26 titles
    Fenno, John Ward (1778-1802), bookseller, New York, N.Y.
    Rivington, James (1724-1802), bookseller, New York, N.Y., & Philadelphia, Pa.

24 titles
    Hall, David (1714-72), bookseller, Philadelphia, Pa.

21 titles
    Bell, Robert (1731?-84), bookseller, Philadelphia, Pa.

20 titles
    Bradford, Thomas (1745-1838), bookseller, Philadelphia, Pa.

19 titles
    Noel, Garrat (fl. 1752-75), & Ebenezer Hazard (1744-1817), booksellers, New York, N.Y.

18 titles
    Noel, Garrat (fl. 1752-75), bookseller, New York, N.Y.

16 titles
    Knox, Henry (1750-1806), bookseller, Boston, Mass.

Architectural Books in Early America

15 titles
  New York, N.Y., Society Library

14 titles
  Baltimore, Md., Library Company
  White, James (1755-1824), bookseller, Boston, Mass.

13 titles
  Thomas, Isaiah (1749-1831), Ebenezer Turrell Andrews (1766-1851), & Obadiah Penniman (1766-1820), booksellers, Albany, N.Y.

12 titles
  Guild, Benjamin (1749-92), bookseller, Boston, Mass.
  Larkin, Ebenezer (1767-1813), bookseller, Boston, Mass.
  Thomas, Isaiah (1749-1831), & Ebenezer Turrell Andrews (1766-1851), booksellers, Boston, Mass.

11 titles
  Campbell, Samuel (1763?-1836), bookseller, New York, N.Y.
  Cox, Edward (fl. 1766-78), & Edward Berry (fl. 1766-72), booksellers, Boston, Mass.

10 titles
  Blake, William Pynson (1769-1820), bookseller, Boston, Mass.
  Blake, William Pynson (1769-1820), & Lemuel (1775-1861), booksellers, Boston, Mass.
  Carey, Mathew (1760-1839), bookseller, Philadelphia, Pa.
  Charleston, S.C., Library Society
  Harvard College Library, Cambridge, Mass.
  West, David (1765-1810), bookseller, Boston, Mass.

9 titles
  Rice, Henry (d. 1804), & Patrick (fl. 1792-1804), booksellers, Philadelphia, Pa.

8 titles
  Newport, R.I., Redwood Library

7 titles
  Hall, William (1752-1834), bookseller, Philadelphia, Pa.
  Philadelphia, Pa., Loganian Library
  Philadelphia, Pa., Union Library Company

6 titles
  Beers, Isaac, (1742?-1813), bookseller, New Haven, Conn.
  Campbell, Robert (d. 1800), bookseller, Philadelphia, Pa.
  Mein, John (fl. 1760-75), bookseller, Boston, Mass.
  Sparhawk, John (1730-1803), bookseller, Philadelphia, Pa.
  Spotswood, William (1753?-1805), bookseller, Boston, Mass., & Philadelphia, Pa.

5 titles
  Allen, Thomas (fl. 1785-99), bookseller, New York, N.Y.
  Rice, Henry (d. 1804), & Company, booksellers, Philadelphia, Pa.
  Thomas, Isaiah (1749-1831), bookseller, Worcester, Mass., Boston, Mass., & Albany, N.Y.

4 titles
  Dunlap, William (d. 1779), bookseller, Philadelphia, Pa.
  Hanover, N.H., Hanover Bookstore
  Larkin, Samuel (1773-1849), bookseller, Portsmouth, N.H.
  Nancrede, Paul Joseph Guérard de (1760-1841), bookseller, Boston, Mass.
  Prichard, William (fl. 1782-1809), bookseller, Philadelphia, Pa.
  Young, William (1755-1829), bookseller, Philadelphia, Pa.

3 titles
  Boston, Mass., broadside, September 30, 1766
  Bradford, William (1719-91), auctioneer, Philadelphia, Pa.

Gaine, Hugh (1726-1807), bookseller, New York, N.Y.
Hudson, Barzillai (1741-1823), & George Goodwin (1757-1844), booksellers, Hartford, Conn.
Providence, R.I., Providence Library
Thomas, Isaiah (1749-1831), Isaiah Thomas, Jr. (1773-1819), & Alexander Thomas (1775-1809), booksellers, Worcester, Mass.

2 titles

Cambell, Duncan (fl. 1693-95), bookseller, Boston, Mass.
Caritat, Louis Alexis Hocquet de (b. 1752), bookseller, New York, N.Y.
Childs, Francis (1763-1830), & Company, booksellers, New York, N.Y.
Clarkson, Matthew (1758-1825), & Ebenezer Hazard (1744-1817), estate administrators, Philadelphia, Pa.
Dabney, John (1752-1819), bookseller, Salem, Mass.
Lancaster, Pa., Juliana Library Company
Payne, Jonas, & Philip Hearn, booksellers, Savannah, Ga.
Philadelphia, Pa., Association Library
Rhode Island College Library [Brown University], Providence, R.I.
Ross, Joseph, & George Douglas, booksellers, Petersburgh, Va.
Stephens, Thomas (fl. 1793-97), bookseller, Philadelphia, Pa.
West, John (1770-1827), bookseller, Boston, Mass.
Yale College Library, New Haven, Conn.

1 title

Albany, N.Y., Albany Library
Arnold, Benedict (1741-1801), druggist & bookseller, New Haven, Conn.
Bradford, William (1719-91), & Thomas (1745-1838), booksellers, Philadelphia, Pa.
Bristol, R.I., Potter Library Company
Burlington, N.J., Library Company
Cox, Thomas (fl. 1733-44), London bookseller, Boston, Mass.

Crukshank, Joseph (1746?-1836), bookseller, Philadelphia, Pa.
Harris, Thaddeus Mason (1768-1842), librarian, Harvard College
Martin, William, bookseller, Boston, Mass.
Moreau de Saint-Méry, Médéric Louis Elie (1750-1819), & Company, booksellers, Philadelphia, Pa.
New York, N.Y., Corporation of the City of New York Library
Russell, Joseph (1734-95), & Samuel Clap (1745-1809, auctioneers, Boston, Mass.
Salem, Mass., Social Library

BIBLIOGRAPHY

Archer, John. *The Literature of British Architecture 1715-1842.* Cambridge, Massachusetts & London, England: The MIT Press, 1985.

Bristol, Roger P. *Supplement to Charles Evans' American Bibliography.* Charlottesville: Published for the Bibliographical Society of America and the Bibliographcal Society of the University of Virginia by the University Press of Virginia, [1970].

Catalog of the Avery Memorial Architectural Library of Columbia University. Second edition. Boston: G. K. Hall, 1968.

Colvin, Howard. *A Biographical Dictionary of British Architects 1600-1840.* London: J. Murray, 1978.

Evans, Charles. *American Bibliography; a Chronological Dictionary of All Books, Pamphlets, and Periodical Publications Printed in the United States of America from the Genesis of Printing in 1639 Down to and Including the Year 1820. With Bibliographical and Biographical Notes.* New York: P. Smith, 1941-59.

The Fowler Architectural Collection of The Johns Hopkins University: Catalogue. Baltimore: Evergreen House Foundation, 1961.

Hitchcock, Henry-Russell. *American Architectural Books: A List of Books, Portfolios, and Pamphlets on Architecture and Related Subjects published in America before 1895.* Revised edition. Minneapolis: University of Minnesota Press, [1962].

Johnston, Phillip M. 'A Checklist of Books Relating to Architecture and the Decorative Arts Available in Philadelphia in the Three Decades Following 1780.' M.A. thesis, University of Delaware, 1974.

Architectural Books in Early America

McCorison, Marcus A. *The 1764 Catalogue of the Redwood Library Company at Newport, Rhode Island.* New Haven: Yale University Press, 1965.

The National Union Catalog, Pre-1956 Imprints. London: Mansell, 1968-

Park, Helen. *A List of Architectural Books Available in America Before the Revolution.* Los Angeles: Hennessey & Ingalls, Inc., 1973.

Shipton, Clifford K, ed. *Early American Imprints, 1639-1800 Series.* Worcester, Mass.: American Antiquarian Society, 1956-

Winans, Robert. *A Descriptive Checklist of Book Catalogues Separately Printed in America 1693-1800.* Worcester: American Antiquarian Society, 1981.

INDEX TO CHECKLIST

Adams, James, 6
Adam, Robert, 6
Albany Library, 44
Alberti, Leone Battista, 6, 27, 80
Allen, Thomas, 47, 53, 68, 125, 139
Ancient architecture, restored, and improved, 74
Ancient buildings of Rome, 24
Ancient masonry, 61
Anderson, James, 6
Andrea Palladio's Elements of architecture, 85
Andrews, Ebenezer Turrell, 8, 12, 17, 20, 21, 65, 67, 71, 93, 97, 106, 110, 112, 116, 118, 146, 149
Architectural remembrancer, 86
Architecture générale de Vitruve, 121
Architecture improved, 86
Architecture of A. Palladio, 78
Architecture of Leon Battista Alberti, 80
Architettura di Leonbatista Alberti, 6
Arnold, Benedict, 139
Art of practical measuring, by the sliding rule, 15
Art of sound building, 34
Association Library Company, see Philadelphia, Pa., Association Library Company
Baltimore, Md., Library Company, 15, 24, 79, 84, 89, 108, 111, 119, 120, 125, 142, 144, 145, 146
Beers, Isaac, 53, 68, 95, 125, 138, 150
Bell, Robert, 9, 19, 37, 51, 58, 61, 64, 66, 68, 72, 76, 77, 78, 82, 86, 101, 121, 140, 147, 153, 158
Benjamin, Asher, 7
Berry, Edward, 28, 43, 48, 54, 64, 66, 69, 76, 148
Blake, Lemuel, 14, 24, 68, 95, 105, 109, 113, 117, 147, 154
Blake, William Pynson, 14, 24, 39, 68, 72, 79, 85, 95, 102, 105, 109, 113, 117, 131, 147, 154
Book of architecture, 31
Boston, Mass., broadside, 39, 82, 103
Bradford, Thomas, 16, 18, 22, 32, 34, 38, 40, 41, 42, 43, 44, 47, 60, 79, 82, 99, 150, 154, 155
Bradford, William, 9, 47, 72, 140
Bristol, R.I., Potter Library Company, 117

British architect: or, the builder's treasury of staircases, 146-47
British carpenter: or, a treatise on carpentry, 124-25
British Palladio,
Brown, Samuel, 12, 16, 29, 32, 33, 36, 38, 40, 43, 46, 49, 52, 58, 59, 63, 71, 73, 77, 87, 89, 102, 104, 128, 133, 136, 137, 138, 141, 152, 160
Builder's chest-book, 62-63
Builder's companion, and workman's general assistant, 102
Builder's compleat assistant, 63-64
Builder's dictionary, 8-9
Builder's director, or bench-mate, 66
Builder's guide, and gentleman and trader's assistant, 135-36
Builder's jewel, 67-68
Builder's pocket-companion, 34-35
Builder's pocket-treasure, 104
Builder's price-book, 12
Burlington, N.J., Library Company, 81
Cambell, Duncan, 27, 56
Campbell, Colin, 13
Campbell, Robert, 47, 53, 96, 105, 113, 148
Campbell, Samuel, 34, 53, 85, 96, 105, 114, 125, 134, 142, 148, 154
Carey, Mathew, 7, 9, 47, 53, 56, 69, 96, 109, 114, 124
Caritat, Louis Alexis Hocquet de, 87, 125
Carpenter and joiner's assistant, 92
Carpenter's and joiner's repository, 107-08
Carpenter's companion: being an accurate and compleat treatise of carpenters works, 144-45
Carpenter's companion for Chinese railing and gates, 18
Carpenter's compleat guide to the whole system of Gothic railing, 83-84
Carpenter's compleat instructor, 153
Carpenter's new guide, 93
Carpenter's pocket directory, 108-09
Carpenters rules of work in the town of Boston, 14
Cash, John, 124
Castell, Robert, 14
Chambers, Sir William, 14, 15
Charleston Library Society, 10, 15, 27, 31, 32, 57, 79, 103, 125, 161
Childs, Francis, 47, 54
Chinese and Gothic architecture properly ornamented, 35
Chinese architecture, civil and ornamental, 22-23
City and country purchaser,

90-91
City and country builder's and workman's treasury of designs, 71-72
Clap, Samuel, 63
Clarkson, Matthew, 26, 156
Coggeshall, Henry, 15, 33
Collection of designs in architecture, containing new plans and elevations of houses, for general use, 150
Columbani, Placido, 16, 17
Compleat body of architecture, 21-22
Compleat measurer adapted to timber and building, 50
Compleat measurer; or, the whole art of measuring, 46
Compleat modern joiner, 157
Compleat tables for measuring round and square timber, 133
Complete body of architecture, 157
Convenient and ornamental architecture, 19
Copland, H., 82
Country builder's assistant, 7
Country builder's estimator, 136-37
Country gentleman's architect, 85-86
Country gentleman's pocket companion, 36
Cox, Edward, 28, 43, 48, 54, 64, 66, 69, 74, 76, 83, 148, 150

Crukshank, Joseph, 48
Crunden, John, 18, 19, 20
Dabney, John, 69, 114
Darly, Matthias, 21
Decker, Paul, 22
De architectura [libri decem], 156
Decorations for parks and gardens, 84
Della architettura di Gio. Antonio Rusconi, 134
Des principes de l'architecture, de la sculpture, de la peinture, 26
Desgodets, Antoine Babuty, 23
Designs, and estimates, of farm houses, 28
Designs for chimney-pieces, 24
Designs for chimnies, 154-55
Designs for shop-fronts and door-cases, 24
Designs in architecture, 145
Designs in carpentry, 153
Designs of Chinese buildings, furniture, dresses, machines, and utensils, 14-15
Designs of Inigo Jones and others published by I: Ware, 158
Designs of Inigo Jones, consisting of plans and elevations for publick and private buildings, 60
Douglas, George, 55, 124
Dunlap, William, 41, 54, 125, 138

Édifices antiques de Rome, 23-24
Elison, Thomas, 84
Espie, François, comte d', 25
Essai sur l'architecture, 77
Essay on architecture, 77
Every man a compleat builder, 98
Falda, Giovanni Battista, 26
Familiar architecture, 130
Félibien, André, 26
Fenno, John Ward, 17, 18, 19, 24, 60, 65, 66, 84, 86, 92, 94, 100, 105, 108, 109, 111, 114, 117, 124, 129, 130, 133, 145, 161, 162
Ferrerio, Pietro, 26
Fires improv'd, 29-30
First book of architecture by Andrea Palladio, 130-31
Four books of Andrea Palladio's architecture, 158
Fréart, Roland, 26
Gaine, Hugh, 69, 126, 148
Garret, Daniel, 28
Gauger, Nicolas, 29
Gentleman and builder's director, 132
Gentleman and farmer's architect, 81-82
Gentleman's and builder's repository, 51
Gentlemens or builders companion, 57
Gibbs, James, 31, 32
Good, John, 33
Goodwin, George, 109, 112

Gothic architecture, 73
Grecian orders of architecture, 131
Grotesque architecture, or, rural amusement, 161-62
Guild, Benjamin, 6, 31, 40, 65, 69, 96, 105, 108, 131, 133, 151, 159
Halfpenny, John, 36, 37, 41, 42
Halfpenny, William, 34, 35, 36, 37, 39, 40, 41, 42, 43, 44
Hall, David, 10, 25, 31, 32, 35, 38, 41, 48, 51, 59, 65, 69, 72, 76, 103, 126, 133, 137, 138, 140, 148, 151, 143, 159
Hall, William, 48, 52, 69, 126, 140, 151, 159
Hanover, N.H., Bookstore, 8, 106, 114, 117
Harris, Thaddeus Mason, 132
Harvard College Library, 6, 13, 15, 79, 119, 121, 134, 143, 156
Hawney, William, 46
Hazard, Ebenezer, 26, 29, 40, 45, 48, 58, 65, 67, 83, 85, 87, 101, 103, 127, 148, 151, 154, 156
Hearn, Philip, 54, 127
Hints for dwellings, 60
Hodgson, Ph. Levi, 50
Hoppus, Edward, 51, 52
Hudson, Barzillai, 109, 112, 120

Hutton, Charles, 56
Hutton, E., 59
Jones, Inigo, 56, 78-79, 155, 157, 158
Jones, William, 57
Jores, J., 58
Joyner and cabinet-maker's darling, 20-21
Juliana Library Company, see Lancaster, Pa., Juliana Library Company
Keay, Isaac, 59
Kent, William, 60, 155
Knox, Henry, 31, 40, 54, 57, 63, 67, 70, 73, 88, 103, 106, 126, 132, 137, 140, 155
Laing, David, 60
Lancaster, Pa., Juliana Library Company, 10, 126
Langley, Batty, 61, 62, 63, 66, 67, 71, 73, 74, 75, 76
Langley, Thomas, 73
Larkin, Ebenezer, 12, 20, 21, 65, 70, 94, 96, 106, 109, 112, 115, 151
Larkin, Samuel, 106, 112, 115, 118
Laugier, Marc Antoine, 77
Le Clerc, Sébastien, 77
Lectures on architecture, 87
Leoni, Giacomo, 78, 80
Leybourn, William, 81
Library Company of Baltimore, see Baltimore, Md., Library Company
Library Company of Burlington, see Burlington, N.J., Library Company
Library Company of Philadelphia, see Philadelphia, Pa., Library Company
Lightoler, Thomas, 37, 81
Lock, Matthias, 82
Loganian Library, see Philadelphia, Pa., Loganian Library
London and country builder's vade mecum, 137
London prices of brick-layers materials and works, 74
Magazine of architecture, perspective & sculpture, 99-100
Mandey, Venterus, 83
Maniere de rendre toutes sortes d'édifices incombustibles, 25
Manner of securing all sorts of buildings from fire, 25
Manwaring, Robert, 83
Martin, William, 157
Measuring made easy, 33-34
Mecanique du feu, 29
Mein, John, 48, 54, 67, 70, 140, 145
Mellificum mensionis: or, the marrow of measuring, 83
Middleton, Charles, 84
Miller, John, 85
Mirror of architecture, 81
Modern builder's assistant, 37
Moreau de Saint-Méry, Médéric Louis Elie, 28
Morris, J. H., 18
Morris, Robert, 37, 86, 87,

88
Morrison, Sir Richard, 89
Most notable antiquity of Great Britain, 56
Moxon, Joseph, 90
Murphy, James, 146
Nancrede, Paul Joseph Guérard de, 17, 70, 115, 118
Narrative of the building and a description of the construction of the Edystone lighthouse with stone, 144
Neve, Richard, 90
New and compleat system of architecture delineated, 39
New book of iron work, 58
New book of ornaments containing a variety of elegant designs for modern pannels, 16
New book of ornaments with twelve leaves, 82
Newport, R.I., Redwood Library, 10, 30, 100, 126, 130, 141, 145, 159
New York, N.Y., Corporation of the City of New York, 28
New York Society Library, 11, 13, 30, 31, 33, 45, 52, 56, 70, 108, 127, 132, 142, 148, 159
Nicholson, Peter, 91, 93
Noel, Garrat, 28, 29, 36, 38, 40, 45, 48, 54, 58, 59, 65, 67, 74, 78, 82, 83, 85, 87, 89, 101, 103, 127, 132, 138, 148, 151, 154

Norman, John, 94
Notes and remarks of Inigo Jones, 78-79
Oakley, Edward, 98, 99
Οἰκίδια, *or, nutshells: being ichnographic distributions for small villas*, 120
Ordonnance des cinq espèces de colonnes selon la méthode des anciens, 121
Ornamental architect, or young-artists instructor, 22
Ornamental architecture, in the Gothic, Chinese and modern taste, 101
Ornamental iron work, 100
Ornaments displayed on a full-size for working, 100
Over, Charles, 101
Pain, William, 102, 104, 107, 108, 110, 113, 116
Pain's British Palladio or, the builder's general assistant, 110-11
Paine, James, 118
Palazzi di Roma de piu celebri architetti, 26
Palladio, Andrea, 78, 85, 119, 130, 158
Palladio Londinensis: or, the London art of building, 138-139
Parallel of the antient architecture with the modern, 27
Parallele de l'architecture antique et de la moderne,

218

26-27
Parallele des anciens et des modems en ce qui regarde les arts et les sciences, 120
Parentalia: or, memoirs of the family of the Wrens, 161
Payne, Jonas, 54, 127
Peacock, James, 120
Penniman, Obadiah, 17, 21, 67, 71, 93, 97, 106, 110, 112, 116, 118, 146, 149
Perrault, Charles, 120, 121
Philadelphia, Pa., Association Library Company, 91, 151
Philadelphia, Pa., Library Company, 6, 7, 11, 13, 14, 20, 25, 30, 32, 33, 45, 57, 60, 62, 75, 79, 80, 91, 112, 120, 122, 127, 141, 142, 143, 144, 145, 146, 149, 151, 159
Philadelphia, Pa., Loganian Library, 30, 73, 90, 91, 120, 131, 157
Philadelphia, Pa., Union Library Company, 49, 62, 80, 91, 122, 123, 127, 152, 160
Picturesque and architectural views for cottages, farm houses, and country villas, 84
Plans, elevations, and sections of buildings, 145-46
Plans, elevations and sections of noblemen and gentlemen's houses, 118-19
Plans, elevations, sections, and views of the church of Batalha, 146
Plaw, John, 123
Pool, Robert, 124
Potter Library Company, see Bristol, R.I., Potter Library Company
Practical architecture, 40-41
Practical builder, or workman's general assistant, 113
Practical geometry, 75
Practical house carpenter, 116-17
Practical measurer, his pocket companion, 59
Practical measuring made easy to the meanest capacity, 52-53
Practical treatise on chimneys, 6
Price, Francis, 124
Prichard, William, 26, 49, 70, 128
Principles of ancient masonry, 61
Principles of bridges, 56
Principles of drawing ornaments made easy, 129
Proportional architecture; or, the five orders, 132
Providence Library, 49, 65, 141
Quattro libri dell'architettura di Andrea Palladio, 119
Ralph, James, 130
Rawlins, Thomas, 130
Redwood Library, see Newport, R.I., Redwood

Library
Regola delli cinque ordini d'architettura, 156
Reigle des cinq ordres d'architecture, 156
Rhode Island College Library, 31, 83
Rice, Henry, 49, 50, 55, 70, 89, 96, 115, 128, 142, 143, 149
Rice, Patrick, 50, 55, 70, 89, 96, 115, 128, 143, 149
Richards, Godfrey, 130
Riou, Stephen, 131
Rivington, James, 11, 12, 16, 23, 29, 32, 33, 36, 38, 40, 43, 44, 46, 49, 52, 58, 59, 63, 71, 73, 77, 87, 89, 101, 102, 103, 104, 128, 133, 136, 137, 138, 141, 152, 160
Robinson, William, 132
Ross, Joseph, 55, 124
Rowland, Thomas, 133
Rudiments of ancient architecture, 133
Rudiments of architecture; or, the young workman's instructor, 134
Rules for drawing the several parts of architecture, 32
Rural architecture: consisting of regular designs of plans and elevations for buildings in the country, 88-89
Rural architecture in the Chinese taste, 41
Rural architecture in the Gothic taste, 42
Rusconi, Giovanni Antonio, 134
Russell, Joseph, 63
Salem, Mass., Social Library, 78
Salmon, William, 135, 136, 137, 138
Select architecture, 88
Semple, George, 141
Series of plans for cottage or habitations of the labourer, 160-61
Serlio, Sebastiano, 143
Several prospects of the most noted publick building, in and about the city of London, 143
Short principles for the architecture of stone-bridges, 131
Smeaton, John, 144
Smith, James, 144
Soane, Sir John, 145
Some designs for buildings both publick and private, 80
Some designs of Mr. Inigo Jones and Mr. Wm. Kent, 155
Sousa Coutinho, Manuel de, 146
Sparhawk, John, 50, 55, 129, 149, 153, 154
Spotswood, William, 50, 55, 97, 115, 129, 149
Stephens, Thomas, 75, 129
Student's instructor in drawing and working the

five orders of architecture, 93-94
Supplement to the British carpenter, 124-25
Swan, Abraham, 146, 150, 153, 154
Thomas, Alexander, 55, 107, 116
Thomas, Isaiah, 8, 12, 17, 20, 21, 55, 65, 67, 71, 93, 97, 106, 107, 109, 110, 112, 115, 116, 118, 138, 146, 149
Thomas, Isaiah, Jr., 55, 107, 116
Theory and practice of architecture, 90
Timber-measure . . . by a double rule, 16
Town and country builder's assistant, 94-95
Traité d'architecture, 77
Treatise of architecture, 78
Treatise of the five orders of columns in architecture, 121
Treatise on building in water, 141-42
Treatise on civil architecture, 15
Tutte l'opere d'architettura di Sebastiano Serlio, 143
Twelve beautiful designs for farm-houses, 43
Twenty new designs of Chinese lattice, 44
Union Library Company, see Philadelphia, Pa., Union Library Company
Upwards of one hundred and fifty new designs, for chimney pieces, 155
Useful and ornamental designs in architecture, 89
Useful architecture in twenty-one new designs, 44
Vardy, John, 155
Variety of capitals, freezes, and corniches, 17-18
Vignola, Giacomo Barozzi, da, 90, 156
Vignola: or the compleat architect, 90
Villas of the ancients illustrated, 14
Vitruvius britannicus, 13
Vitruvius Pollio, 156
Wallis, N., 157
Ware, Isaac, 157, 158
West, David, 8, 21, 66, 71, 97, 107, 110, 112, 116, 118
West, John, 107, 116
White, James, 18, 20, 24, 25, 56, 84, 93, 94, 107, 110, 113, 116, 118, 157
Wood, John, 160
Workman's golden rule, 76
Works in architecture of Robert and James Adam, 6
Wren, Sir Christopher, 161
Wrighte, William, 161
Yale College Library, 80, 91
Young, William, 81, 97, 150, 153